An Illustrated History
of
GLASGOW'S RAILWAYS

C000280719

Glasgow has benefitted from intense suburban passenger services for nearly a century and a quarter. Typical of such trains in early BR days was Stanier 2–6–2 tank No.40185 with the 1.30 pm from Paisley St. James to Glasgow St. Enoch, arriving at Shields Road on 11th April 1958. Tenements such as those in Seaward Street behind the engine formed a backdrop to many railway scenes in the city.

W.A.C. Smith and Paul Anderson

Copyright Irwell Press 1993
ISBN 1-871608-33-3
Printed by Amadeus Press, Huddersfield
First published in UK by Irwell Press, 15 Lovers Lane, Grasscroft, OLDHAM OL4 4DP.

IRWELL
PRESS

CONTENTS

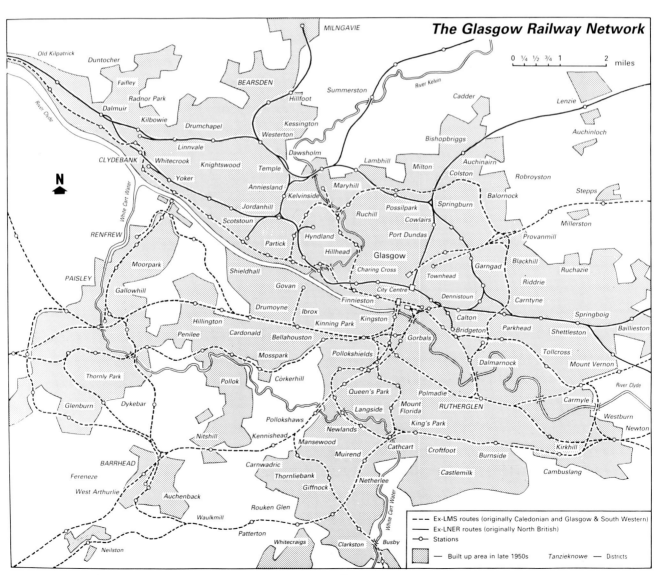

The Glasgow Railway Network

--- Ex-LMS routes (originally Caledonian and Glasgow & South Western)
— Ex-LNER routes (originally North British)
–○– Stations
░ Built up area in late 1950s   *Tanzieknowe* — Districts

Glasgow and its Railways

One of the drawbacks facing photographers of Glasgow's railways or any other outdoor subject for that matter was the climate. A steady downpour from moist westerly winds hitting the hills was a common occurrence and even when the rain held off a cloying damp mist often gripped the city. Such were the conditions on 22nd August 1962 as Fairburn 2–6–4 tank No.42204 made a lusty start from Rutherglen with the 5.50 pm Glasgow Central – Motherwell local and overhauled Standard 5MT 4–6–0 No.73072, drifting along with a rake of LMS–designed corridor stock. An industrial backdrop peered through the gloom above the triangular station – a second set of platforms stood beyond the carriage sidings and a third was off to the right, both fed by the line from Dalmarnock and Central Low Level.

Love it or loath it, Glasgow cannot be ignored for there is nowhere like the city on the Clyde. It's a place of contradictions for a start. The finest assemblage of Victorian architecture in the world made up the central area, yet some of the worst slum housing of any industrial country blighted the inner suburbs. Glasgow built most of the world's ships and locomotives for many years but some of the yards and factories became a hotbed of militancy and communism. Strangers were assured a very generous if sometimes incomprehensible welcome, yet the city gained a reputation for vicious gang warfare. Persistent rain and clinging fog are familiar aspects of the climate but there is an horrific history of fires and many of the station buildings featured in this book have suffered that fate. The contradictions even extended to railways. In the 1950s there was a wonderful range of steam engines at work, yet local interest was minimal and the little group on the end of the platform at Central was quite probably made up of English enthusiasts. Glasgow's railway system was incredibly varied and grew up over a 70–year period. It included one of Scotland's pioneering lines and the most expensive sub–surface suburban route ever built. Two famous city centre terminus stations received expresses from south of the border but certain suburban termini were little known, even by those with considerable knowledge of railways. Much of the system is intact and electrified today so Glasgow has a very high proportion of commuters who travel by rail, despite the continuing lack of local enthusiasts.

From the lofty slopes of Cairn Table in the Southern Uplands the River Clyde tumbles down past Symington and Lanark to the Clydesdale gorge. It emerges at Dalserf and wanders across the fringe of the great wedge of Coal Measure rocks stretching from Wishaw and Coatbridge to Falkirk, which proved so vital to the economy of central Scotland. Eventually the river widens out to become the glorious Firth of Clyde. To the south, tough volcanic rocks form the harsh heights of Cunninghame and Hill of Stake whilst to the north the long–cooled basalt lava flows are responsible for the Kilpatrick Hills and Campsie Fells. Beyond them the wild and beautiful Highlands begin with Loch Lomond and its associated Ben. In the once heavily forested basin between Clydesdale and the sea Glasgow began in a modest way thirteen centuries ago. Even earlier the Romans made a brief visit and discovered a tribe they called *Celtic Damnonii*, who despite their heathen nature were clearly so enthralled with one particular spot by the Clyde that they called it 'Dear Green Place' which was later corrupted to 'Glasgow' – or so legend has it! Very little happened alongside the sparkling salmon river until the late 600s when St. Mungo was sent from the east coast to convert the barbarians of Strathclyde to Christianity. He built a monastery near the tiny Molendinar Burn, the influence of the church spread, and the seeds were set which would lead to the growth of one of the world's great cities.

In 1015 the kingdom of Strathclyde became part of Scotland. A wooden cathedral was built in 1136 only to burn down 50 years later, by which time Glasgow was significant enough to be called a city. The present splendid but gloomy edifice was begun in 1174 and there was a mention of Glasgow Green about the same time. Nearby towns, now totally overshadowed by the city, were far more important in the past. Rutherglen for instance was made a royal burgh 500 years before Glasgow and the Scottish parliament was sitting there in 1300. Medieval times saw progress at the expense of these neighbours however, especially following the establishment of the University amid the timber and thatch cottages of High Street in 1451. Nearby Provands Lordship, a stone house built for the priest in charge of St. Nicholas hospital, dates from 1471 and is now a museum. Glasgow consolidated its role as a thriving cathedral and university city during the 1500s and for a while it was not affected by the turbulent Reformation elsewhere. But religious bigotry eventually resulted in violence and together with the rest of Scotland, Glasgow was firmly Protestant by 1560. Reformation was never popular with the Scottish monarchs and the ensuing turmoil led to the famous Battle of Langside where Mary Queen of Scots was routed, fleeing south only to be executed by Elizabeth I at Fotheringay Castle in Northamptonshire.

Nevertheless England and Scotland were drawing closer together and the 'Union of Crowns' came in 1606. Meanwhile Glasgow was flourishing. Guilds of merchants and craftsmen were established, Saltmarket and Gallowgate became extremely prosperous and the population reached 8000. At last the city became a royal burgh and in 1636 the stark Tolbooth tower was erected as a reminder that

Last train to Bellahouston. Ex-Caledonian Railway McIntosh 0–4–4 tank No.55211 headed into the sunset with the 5.46 pm from Glasgow St. Enoch to Paisley West on 18th September 1954, calling at this suburban station immediately prior to its closure.

visitors arriving at Glasgow Cross had to pay a fee. Times were not always easy – in 1647 plague ravaged the city and in 1652 fire destroyed a third of Glasgow's houses. However, there were already hints of the trading role that would transform Clydeside. An illicit shipment of tobacco arrived in 1674 from Virginia – one of England's prized colonies in America – and merchants watched their ships arrive from the Briggait Steeple. Down below, life was more mundane. Drinking was banned in public taverns after 10 pm and throwing excrement on to the streets was prohibited in 1696. The Act of Union between Scotland and England in 1707 set the seal on the future of Glasgow. At first people rioted against it, but it paved the way towards an economic base to take full advantage of the industrial revolution and created the second city of the Empire. By 1726 there were 50 sailing boats plying legally to Virginia and New England. Imported sugar was being baked to produce molasses for Glasgow brandy and cotton was used to make linen and muslin. Tobacco was paramount and the 'Tobacco Lords' built sumptuous mansions, socialised in 'Gentlemen's Clubs' and introduced banking to the west of Scotland.

Two modest yet very significant events which set the scene for Glasgow's growth as a great railway city occurred in the mid–18th century. In 1750 John Dixon opened a horse-operated waggonway from his Knightswood coal pits to the Clyde at Yoker and in 1765 James Watt thought of the idea of a separate condenser for improving mine steam engines while walking across Glasgow Green. At this time the city had a population of 28,000 but by 1791 it had reached 67,000, swelled by High-

landers attracted by the rapidly growing cotton and iron industries. Meanwhile *The Glasgow Herald* had been formed in 1783, George Square was laid out on marshland in 1787 and the Forth & Clyde Canal opened in 1790. The new 'Merchant City' east of George Square with its gems of Georgian architecture was started in the early 1800s as was the first part of the Gorbals, a byword for bad housing for much of its life but a prosperous suburb at first. Still the industrial base strengthened. In 1800 Sir Charles Tennant established his chemical works at St. Rollox which managed to spread noxious smoke over the city even after its 436 feet chimney was erected. More rails were laid in 1811 when William Dixon built a waggonway from Govanhill to convey coal to the Ardrossan Canal basin at Port Eglinton, but the following year there was an event of enormous significance with the launch of the COMET, the Clyde's first commercially successful steamboat.

Steam engines and rails finally came together in 1831 when the Garnkirk & Glasgow Railway opened its line from the Monklands coalfield to a sizeable goods yard and impoverished passenger station near the chemical works at St. Rollox. By this time the city was home to some 200,000 people, many of them Irish immigrants, and a startling rise in the iron industry was underway. Neilson & Co – the first firm founded in Glasgow specifically to build locomotives – started at Hyde Park Street in Finnieston during 1836, moving to Springburn in 1862. In the west end work began on the magnificent crescents of Park Circus and Park Terrace overlooking Kelvingrove Park, and Great Western Road had just

been laid out providing a grand approach from Dumbarton. In the centre, notably around Argyle Street, the squalid back streets of ramshackle houses known as the 'Wynds' were rife with filth and crime as well as the occasional outbreak of cholera. However, another landmark in the history of Glasgow was the construction of the first workers' tenements in 1830, for these dour blocks eventually became one of the hallmarks of the city.

At a time when the potato famine was leading to a massive influx of Irish looking for work, Glasgow gained two important railways from out of town, heralding an even greater expansion of industry. The line from Paisley and beyond which reached Bridge Street in 1840 improved communications with the Clyde Coast enormously, whilst the Edinburgh & Glasgow Railway of 1842 was Scotland's first trunk line and penetrated the city centre at Queen Street. It later became part of the North British Railway empire. There was less optimism in the back streets where conditions were becoming even worse, encouraging the rich to move out to fine terraces at Charing Cross, Hillhead and around the newly created Botanic Gardens. In 1848 the Caledonian Railway completed its line from Carlisle, then in 1849 Buchanan Street station opened and Queen Victoria passed through Queen Street on her way to Balmoral. At the same time Glasgow had one of the worst infant mortality rates in Europe with smallpox rife and half the children dying before they reached five. The poor existed on porridge, sheep's heads and pig's trotters and even then there were hunger-induced 'Bread Riots' on Glasgow Green, the military shooting people dead.

Maritime trade and shipbuilding were crucial to the growth of Glasgow. In 1802 the first ever steamboat, CHARLOTTE DUNDAS, was built at Bowling and in 1812 the same yard launched the COMET. This proved to be the first commercially successful steamer in the world and a replica of it proudly sailed up the Clyde on 15th October 1962, during 150th anniversary celebrations for this momentous event. In the background the freighter CINDERELLA unloaded grain at Meadowside Quay which was built by the Clyde Navigation Trust just before World War 1. Other significant years for the River Clyde included 1818 when the first iron ship VULCAN was launched, 1840 when Cunard was formed to provide regular trans–Atlantic services and created a huge demand for ships, 1879 when the first steel ship was built at Dumbarton and 1946 when the last sea–going paddle steamer WAVERLEY was built.

George Square in the centre of Glasgow displayed several features characteristic of the city. Municipal pride was clearly demonstrated by the statues, monuments and above else by the magnificent council chambers. The thorough penetration of railways into the central area was typified by Queen Street station in the left background of this view. However, probably the most famous Glasgow institution ever was the fleet of 'caurs' which constantly whined and clattered through streets far and wide for over 60 years. Corporation Standard trams Nos.73 and 12 bound for Scotstoun West and Dalmarnock respectively passed in George Square on 5th March 1960.

Caledonian motive power in the Glasgow area comprised a collection of 0–4–2 tender and 2–4–0 tank engines at first, supplemented by the 2–4–2Ts intended unsuccessfully for the Oban line. Then came the small Drummond 0–4–4Ts for local services, followed by Lambie 4–4–0Ts for the Central Low Level system. From 1900 the more powerful McIntosh '439' class 0–4–4Ts were used extensively on suburban work and a final batch of them was turned out as late as 1925 by the LMS. The ubiquitous 'Jumbo' 0–6–0s built over a period of 15 years were also employed on passenger services and the larger '812' variant of 1899/1900 saw frequent use on the fast Clyde Coast boat trains. Then there were Pickersgill's huge 4–6–2Ts dating from World War 1 which were used for a time on the Wemyss Bay and Edinburgh routes. For much of the Caley's existence, long distance workings were handled by a succession of 4–4–0s and 4–6–0s including the famous 'Dunalastair' and 'Cardean' classes. Pickersgill 4–4–0 No.54461, one of the less heralded examples, had been relegated to working locals such as the 4.3 pm Lanark to Glasgow Central on 11th May 1954. It took on water at Eglinton Street (but only a small proportion of that coming out of the crane it seems!) prior to a stint on Cathcart Circle duties. The 'bow tie' above the buffer beam is the inherited Caledonian route indicator for the Carlisle main line and its branches.

Glasgow & South Western motive power consisted almost entirely of a succession of fairly modest tender locos. One of these, a four–cylinder 4–4–0 designed by James Manson, emerged from Kilmarnock Works in 1897 as No.11. This particular engine was completely rebuilt with a large boiler by R.H.Whitelegg in 1922 and given the name LORD GLENARTHUR after the last chairman of the G & SW. It was an impressive sight and worked for a time on Glasgow – Ayr expresses along with Whitelegg's six massive 4–6–4 'Baltic' tanks also introduced during 1922. The latter came as something of a surprise considering the Sou'West's penchant for tenders. During 1923 LORD GLENARTHUR became No.14509 in the LMS fleet and proudly carried that company's crimson livery and crest. The engine is seen in this form at St. Enoch with a train of Midland designed coaches in matching colours. However, the former G & SW loco stock in general was a motley collection of ageing machines, soon replaced by sprightly Derby designed 2P 4–4–0s. No.14509 itself finished its days in plain black and the end came in 1934. Photograph courtesy Neville Stead.

Although the 1850s were a quiet time for railway construction, other developments were starting to influence the character of the city. Fresh Highland water was piped from Loch Katrine in mid decade and soon helped counter cholera and other diseases. Caledonia Road church, one of the first of Alexander 'Greek' Thomson's beautiful classical contributions to the city skyline, appeared in 1856. So too did John Baird's iron framed Gardner's Warehouse on Jamaica Street which not only proved to be a landmark in European architecture but heralded the explosion of Victorian 'temples of commerce' which were to transform the central area. By the time the bucolic railway from Cowlairs to Maryhill, Dumbarton and Helensburgh opened in 1858 Glasgow was becoming recognised as the second city of the Empire. Over the following ten years only relatively minor branch lines were built – Milngavie 1863, Busby 1866 and Govan 1868 – but again the city itself was undergoing relentless economic growth, with the Clyde featuring strongly. Shipyards were launching a total of 100,000 tons per annum, Broomielaw and Windmillcroft Quays became jammed with trading vessels, and racing by passenger steamers to the estuary towns was rife. In 1866 the new coat of arms, featuring a robin in a tree and a salmon with a ring from the St. Mungo legend, shortened the patron saint's 'Let Glasgow flourish by the preaching of the word' to 'Let Glasgow Flourish' – and it did. The formation of Queen's Park Football Club in 1867 followed shortly afterwards by Rangers and Celtic was another landmark that can hardly be disputed!

Glasgow's population reached 500,000 by 1869 and there had been a pressing need for better rail transport for some time. As a result the following decade saw a series of major schemes come to fruition and they established the basic pattern still recognisable today. In 1870 the City of Glasgow Union Railway bridged the Clyde and linked existing lines either side of the river. During 1871 trains began to run from Coatbridge to College station, which took over the medieval site of the University when it moved to the west end. The first commuter service started the same year with 'bus trains' running between Bellgrove and Shields Road over the College and City Union lines. In 1874 a modest but significant branch from the Helensburgh line curved its way down to new docks at Stobcross whilst during 1876 the mighty terminus at St. Enoch began to take shape and Glasgow acquired London expresses from St. Pancras (over the Glasgow and South Western route) as well as those from Euston via the Caledonian Railway. The latter arrived at the new Central station over a second Clyde bridge from 1879. In some ways the city continued to reflect its rural past at this time, for cattle were still grazing on Glasgow Green in 1870. In other ways there were pointers to the future, particularly the tartan horse–drawn tram which Andrew Menzies inaugurated between St. George's Cross and Eglinton Toll in 1872. By the 1880s Glasgow was supremely confident as a result of its success and wealth and this was reflected in the municipal magnificence of the City Chambers overlooking George Square. No expense was spared celebrating the city's prosperity with

dazzling mosaics, marble pillars and intricate tapestries. Queen Victoria opened this extravaganza in 1888 and visited the International Exhibition at Kelvingrove at the same time. Entertainment as far as the working population was concerned centred around music halls, and Harry Lauder made his first appearance at the Scotia Theatre in 1887 only to be told to go home and practice by the manageress. Not everyone was content with the triumphs of commerce and in the late 1880s Kier Hardie and his colleagues were determined to overthrow the capitalist system, thus setting the seeds for a vibrant aspect of Glasgow's history during the next century. Meanwhile a railway to the growing shipbuilding community of Clydebank opened in 1882, the first part of the celebrated Cathcart Circle was completed during 1886, and an underground suburban line linking the east and west ends of the city via a low level station at Queen Street opened in the same year.

Thirty years of relentless tenement building had made Glasgow one of the most densely populated and compact cities in the world by 1890. But surrounding settlements had also grown and the municipal boundary was extended in 1891 by the absorption of Govanhill, Crosshill, Pollokshields, Hillhead, Maryhill, Mount Florida, Langside, Shawlands, Kelvinside, Possilpark and Springburn. Reconstruction of the city centre proceeded apace at the same time and produced a whole series of magnificent facades, many of them the inspiration of local architects. The new Glasgow Herald Building of 1895 was a good example and a young draughtsman called Charles Rennie

North British local passenger services were in the hands of outclassed 0–4–2 well tanks until these were replaced by 0–6–0 saddle tanks in the early 1870s. Then came the Drummond side tanks, virtually an enlarged Stroudley Terrier design bearing the names of places served – PARTICK and BELLGROVE for example – and large 4–4–0Ts for Helensburgh expresses. All of these were eventually ousted by Holmes 4–4–0s and 0–4–4Ts. Under W.P. Reid an order for thirty 4–4–2Ts was completed in 1913, soon followed by 21 superheated engines and these took over Glasgow suburban duties. In its twilight days class C16 4–4–2T No.67500, dating from 1921, was employed as station pilot at Bridgeton Central on 15th February 1958.

Mackintosh was involved in its design. Eventually he became one of the most famous names associated with the city, but not before disaffection and resentment set in and caused him to leave. His legacy includes the beautiful Willow Tea Room in Sauchiehall Street, St. Matthews church at Queen's Cross, Scotland Street School, and of course the enormously original Glasgow School of Art. Concurrently new suburban and underground railways were taking up a lot of money. The Cathcart Circle was completed in 1894 and the cable–worked Subway together with the vastly expensive Central Low Level line below Argyle Street opened in 1896. All three featured excellent buildings by Glasgow architects. Competition for suburban steam trains was stirring however. In 1894 Glasgow Corporation took over the city's tramways and soon decided to electrify them, whilst in 1899 the Albion Car Company was formed.

No less than 100,000 tenements had been built by 1900 and they formed much of the fabric of the city and its suburbs. Up to the early 1890s they were faced with grey or golden blocks from Giffnock a few miles to the south, but when this ran out the red sandstone of Dumfries and Arran was employed. City centre Edwardian opulence reached bloated levels in 1907 when the Grosvenor Building opposite Central station received an additional storey featuring muscular men and ample breasted maidens supporting the eaves high above street level and thus hardly noticed by anyone! This decade was the zenith of Glasgow's confidence and it began with the second International Exhibition at Kelvingrove during 1901 which was even more ambitious and successful than the first. Self assurance was also a feature of the railways. Central station underwent a massive rebuilding programme which was completed in 1905 whilst the North British Locomotive Company was formed in 1903 out of existing firms with the intention of supplying an even greater proportion of the world's railway engines – which it did abundantly for over half a century. Sadly the huge bubble representing Glasgow's industrial success story was ready to burst and there were ominous signs that the railways had reached the peak of their development as well. The intensive Springburn – Govan 'bus train' service was abandoned in 1902 and a series of lavish Caledonian suburban stations between Paisley and Barrhead were built shortly afterwards but never opened. Govan, Partick, Pollokshaws, Shettleston, Tollcross, Cathcart, Dawsholm, Temple and Knightswood were absorbed by Glasgow in 1912. Meanwhile shipbuilding had become an enormous industry and no less than ¾ million tons was launched in 1913 with 60,000 men employed in numerous yards. World War 1 resulted in an upheaval in Glasgow as elsewhere, with some thirty yards turning out ships for the war effort and women in long tartan skirts taking over as tram conductresses. A large number of local stations closed for normal passenger traffic in 1917, although most of them remained open for essential workmens' services and reopened for public trains two years later. Militancy was also a feature of the war years with Jimmy Maxton making his anti–war speech on Glasgow Green. He was promptly arrested but his Independent Labour Party organised a shipyard strike and made Glasgow the natural focus of worker agitation. In 1919 police and striking miners clashed violently in George Square. The city's tenements were also becoming a problem and the 1918 Royal Commission on Housing decided that new council houses on peripheral farmland were the only answer to the stock of overcrowded and decaying apartments.

At leisure, Glasgow clearly enjoyed the 1920s with over 50 Palais de Danse vibrating with the new Charleston and Foxtrot. Outside, the textile industry was being squeezed out by Lancashire mills and foreign competition, Lanarkshire coal was suffering a dramatic decline, and ironmaking was dealt a dramatic blow when Stewarts & Lloyds moved to Corby in Northamptonshire, taking many of their employees with them. In the 1922 General Election ten out of fifteen Glasgow seats were won by the Independent Labour Party and the 'Red Clydesiders', including Manny Shinwell, were cheered by thousands of supporters as they boarded the overnight train from St. Enoch. Inevitably they proved lively MPs and sometimes pushed the House beyond the breaking point of its tolerance. Back on Clydeside the mix of Protestants, Irish Catholics, unemployment, bad housing and militancy was causing considerable social problems including growing gang warfare. The railways carried on much as before – apart from the premature withdrawal of the Govan branch service in 1921 – until the Grouping of 1923. The Caledonian and Glasgow & South Western then became part of the vast London Midland & Scottish Railway with the North British absorbed by the London & North Eastern Railway (LMS and LNER respectively).

Shipbuilding in Glasgow, once one of the keystones of the Scottish economy and a huge source of vessels worldwide, was in deep trouble during the 1930s – mainly because of the recession and foreign competition. The famous Cunarder QUEEN MARY languished as a half built rusting hulk at John Brown's yard in Clydebank until government help led to its launch during 1933. Furthermore the despair of the city was not helped by two novels published during 1935. George Blake's *The Shipbuilders* portrayed scenes of redundant men gazing silently at derelict berths where they once tugged off their caps and cheered as a new liner left the keel blocks and settled in the Clyde. The other was more damaging and gave rise to a slur which stuck. Alexander McArthur's *No Mean City* told a terrible story of drunkenness, poverty, moral corruption and brutality in the teeming tenements. It also glorified the hatchet, bicycle chain and razor gangs of Calton, Bridgeton and Gorbals. Glasgow has always had its 'wee hard men' but the reputation for violence was never totally justified and cities elsewhere in the world had far worse records.

On a happier note the city boasted the largest cinema in Europe, the QUEEN ELIZABETH was launched in 1938 with no delay, and housing schemes such as the garden suburbs of Knightswood, Mosspark, Cardonald and Carntyne were replacing the worst slums. By 1939 over 20% of the city's population lived in council houses. At the outbreak of World War 2 there were still almost thirty steamers offering trips 'doon the watter'. They were divided between the LMS Caledonian Steam Packet fleet, distinguished by yellow funnels, the associated Williamson–Buchanan Steamers Ltd (with white funnels), the LNER paddlers with their red funnels bearing a white band, MacBrayne vessels with red funnels and the Clyde and Campbeltown Shipping Co., sporting black funnels with broad red band. Soon many of them would be wearing camouflage grey and engaged in minesweeping operations off the east coast, from the Firth of Forth to the Thames. Glasgow received a significant

In LMS days the underpowered Stanier 2-6-2Ts were an unpopular import to the Glasgow area for suburban duties although the big Fowler 2–6–4Ts which arrived about the same time were well liked and used until after nationalisation. Soon after World War 2 batches of Fairburn 2–6–4Ts were introduced, followed by the BR Standard variant from 1951 and these continued until the last years of steam. Main line services saw successive builds of LMS express engines. Stanier 'Coronation' Pacific No.6228 DUCHESS OF RUTLAND was an impressive sight at Glasgow Central on 12th July 1938 having arrived with the down 'Royal Scot'. Photograph J.P.Wilson.

boost during the conflict with over 300 ships built on the Clyde from 1939 to 1945 and 80% of UK imports coming through its docks. Sadly there was also a shipping tragedy when the liner ATHENIA was sunk on its way from Glasgow to Canada with evacuees right at the beginning of the war. The city itself escaped large scale bombing so the Victorian heritage and railway system alike remained virtually unscathed. But from 13th to 15th March 1941 Clydebank was targeted with a vengeance and over a thousand of its inhabitants were killed. Railway casualties were limited to station closures in the west end – Botanic Gardens and Kirklee in 1939 and Kelvinside in 1942. A positive development in these troubled times was the foundation of the Citizens Theatre in 1942 which was a hint of the cultural revolution four decades later. A less successful herald of change was the Clyde Valley Plan of 1946 which led to massive slum clearances but resulted in social problems in new estates on the outskirts. The LMS and LNER became part of the nationalised British Railways, as its Scottish Region, in 1948.

No less than 80,000 tenements were swept away during the 1950s and 1960s. Districts such as Gallowgate and Gorbals lost row after row of stalwart sandstone blocks with their familiar tiled or painted entrance closes, one or two room apartments, sometimes devoid of plumbing, and 'cludgies' in back courts or on landings. Despite the Saturday night shouting and daytime din from weans playing, fighting or crying in the streets or courts, these were cohesive communities and they were ruthlessly dismantled. Working class Glaswegians could put up with appalling housing, poverty and even violence but many found it hard to come to terms with some of the new estates. Glasgow's pioneering pre–war 'schemes' had worked quite well, but the municipal sprawls at Nitshill, Pollok, Drumchapel and Castlemilk soon ran into difficulties. Easterhouse, one of the most desperate of all, was built without shops, pubs, schools, libraries, or cinemas. By 1960 the Corporation had run out of peripheral land and started to put up tower blocks where the tenements had been, but many of these became troublesome as well. The city's faltering self confidence was not helped by its declining industrial base, dramatically illustrated by the collapse of the Fairfield shipyard in Govan during 1965. Two years later the QE2 became the last of a long line of great passenger liners to be launched on the Clyde. During the 1950s Glasgow's railways were still almost wholly steam–worked and retained most of their original facilities, the only losses being a handful of inner suburban stations such as Kelvinbridge, Glasgow Green and Stobcross. The 1960s saw tremendous changes however with the completion of the North Side and South Side electrification schemes in 1960 and 1962 respectively, the closure of most ex-–Caledonian passenger and goods lines north of the river, including the Central Low Level route during 1964/66, the end of St. Enoch and Buchanan Street main line termini in 1966, and the conclusion of the Clyde Coast electrification works together with the elimination of steam during 1967.

During the early 1970s there was continuing frustration in Glasgow as shipbuilding declined further, resulting in a 'sit–in' organised by Jimmy Reid when Upper Clyde Shipbuilders went bankrupt during 1971. Such was the success of this protest that government money was forthcoming to create the new Govan Shipbuilders. An era really did come to an end in 1974 when WAVERLEY – the last Clyde paddle steamer – was sold by the Scottish Transport Group, although it continued to run trips under private ownership. Another fundamental change in transport philosophy was reflected by councillors who enthused over the transformation of Glasgow into the 'motor-way city' with the completion of Kingston Bridge and the M8 through Charing Cross in 1971. A year later the Greater Glasgow Passenger Transport Executive was formed and soon set about altering the distinctive orange, pale green and cream colours which had adorned the corporation trams and buses for so long. Another shake up took place during 1975 when local government reorganisation made Glasgow part of the Strathclyde Region. Back in 1971 there had been a faint glimmer of the renaissance of the city when a conservation report concluded that it had the finest Victorian heritage in Europe. Following this, GEAR (Glasgow Eastern Area Renewal) was launched in 1976 and a programme of refurbishing the remaining tenements and cleaning city centre buildings was inaugurated. Meanwhile BR was still recovering from the Beeching mayhem a decade earlier and displayed a bland blue and grey corporate livery, but morale was given a boost with the completion of the West Coast electrification to Glasgow Central on 6th May 1974. Clydeside made its own contribution to rail revival with the reopening of the Central Low Level route in 1979 and a startling transformation of the old Subway into an ultra–modern tube line at the same time.

With a lot of effort and a change of fortune Glasgow finally began to regain its self confidence during the 1980s. The large yet rather erratic Burrell collection donated to his native city by ship owner Sir William Burrell was finally displayed in a specially built museum at Pollok House from 1983. This proved to be the first thrust of the new Glasgow, but almost simultaneously the vastly successful 'Glasgow's Miles Better' campaign identified by Mr Happy and helped by £1 million from the private sector was launched. The wide ranging Mayfest Arts Festival reflecting a new cultural confidence also began in 1983 and five years

Under LNER management a number of class N2 0–6–2Ts of Great Northern Railway origin were transferred to the Glasgow area during the 1920s but they were both unpopular with crews and unkind to the track. However, the Gresley V1 2–6–2Ts which arrived from 1930 onwards proved to be extremely competent performers and they monopolised residential traffic on the former North British routes for thirty years. B1 4–6–0s gradually replaced the earlier 4–4–0s whilst Pacifics – particularly Gresley A3s from Haymarket shed – were frequently found on Queen Street – Edinburgh expresses. In later years Leeds Holbeck A3s worked over the G & SW route as well. On Sunday 3rd July 1960 No.60080 DICK TURPIN departed from Glasgow St. Enoch with the up 'Thames – Clyde Express'.

later the International Garden Festival was held on land reclaimed from Prince's Dock east of Govan. However, when Glasgow was designated European City of Culture for 1990 Edinburgh was taken aback, many Clydesiders were amazed, and Billy Connolly and Rab C Nesbitt had a new avenue of humour to pursue. Deeper consideration showed that by then the city fully deserved this accolade. In 1980 responsibility for local transport passed from Greater Glasgow PTE to a new Strathclyde PTE. Initially the Regional Council seemed to be more interested in running express buses than trains and a secret report proposed drastic line closures. Fortunately sense prevailed and the strong orange and black livery applied to trains and buses alike from 1985 was accompanied by a more balanced approach. Both the 'Strathclyde Rail Review' of 1987 and the 1990 document 'Public Transport for the 21st Century' proposed an expansion of the rail network.

The Glasgow of the 1990s is very different to that of forty years ago. Its population is less than 700,000 compared with 1,120,000 just after World War 2, and is still declining slowly. Only 55,000 people are now employed in manufacturing, but some 22,000 work in tourism and there are no less than 60,000 students at local universities and colleges. The city centre and west end are very smart whilst Govan and the east end are improving, but several peripheral estates have too many people alienated both economically and socially from the city's revival. Most of the 21.5% male unemployment is in these areas and there are third generation out of work in some families. One of the most ironic developments is the decision to demolish 1960s tower blocks in Hutchesontown and Gorbals and replace them with modern four storey tenements! Fortunately in 1993 Glasgow retained a superb suburban railway system and had a higher percentage of the local population regularly travelling into town by train than any other British city. There were also firm commitments to reintroduce passenger services to the Rutherglen – Coatbridge route, the central section of the City of Glasgow Union line through St. Johns, and the Northern Suburban link via Maryhill and Possil. If government policy is not to force everyone to travel by private car or deregulated bus, these schemes should come to fruition and flourish. However, it is not the intention of this book to speculate on the future but to celebrate the past, to illustrate it with scenes from the 1950s and early 1960s when most Victorian railway infrastructure was intact, privatisation was unheard of, and Glasgow was still decidedly grimy!

Glasgow's 'Blue Trains' were one of the most distinctive designs ever on British Railways. Apart from the bright Kingfisher livery they had interiors clearly reflecting the 'contemporary' look of the late 1950s and early 1960s. The colour contrasts were remarkable. Deep red upholstery against bright yellow panels featured in one section of the centre coach, whilst the ends of the outer cars with their panoramic views had striped brown moquette seats and pale grey formica with a fussy little triangular pattern. But a design fault in the switchgear put the whole fleet out of action for nearly a year. On 6th November 1960, the first day of the full north side electric service, the 1.41 pm from Springburn to Milngavie rolled into Barnhill. Maybe the headcode 56 was a hint of things to come. It signified the unlikely Singer Works via Yoker stopping and should have read 65, indicating Springburn – Milngavie!

After a period when new and refurbished Clydeside electric units featured yellow interiors and tiny blue seats, the class 320 multiple units delivered in 1990 could once again be called native Glaswegians. The old 'Blue Train' comfort returned with a much improved seat design and the bulkhead panels were adorned with reproductions of drawings specially commissioned from four members of the Glasgow School of Art. Subjects included the 'Comet', People's Palace, Cathedral, University, Scotland Street School and, of course, the School of Art itself. On 24th April 1991 unit 320 303 paused at Glasgow Queen Street Low Level with the 10.24 from Helensburgh to Airdrie. Photograph Paul Anderson.

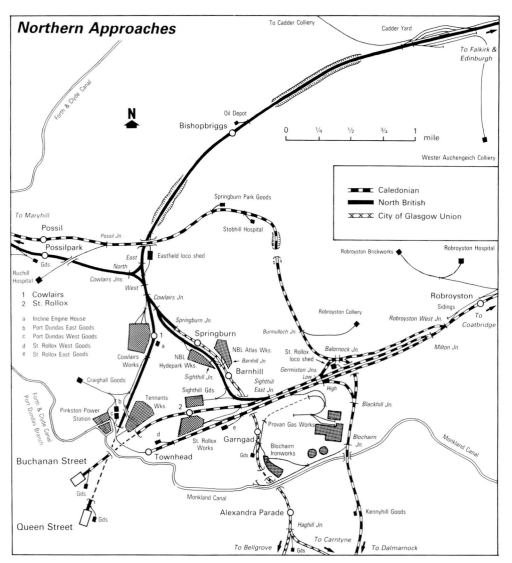

Northern Approaches

To Cadder Colliery

Cadder Yard

To Falkirk & Edinburgh

Forth & Clyde Canal

N

Oil Depot

Bishopbriggs

0 ¼ ½ ¾ 1 mile

Wester Auchengeich Colliery

Caledonian
North British
City of Glasgow Union

Springburn Park Goods

Robroyston Brickworks   Robroyston Hospital

To Maryhill

Possil

Possilpark   Possil Jn.

Stobhill Hospital

Ruchill   Gds.   Eastfield loco shed
Hospital   East
North   Cowlairs Jns.
West
Cowlairs Jn.

Robroyston
Sidings
To
Coatbridge

Robroyston West Jn.

1   Cowlairs
2   St. Rollox
a   Incline Engine House
b   Port Dundas East Goods
c   Port Dundas West Goods
d   St Rollox West Goods
e   St Rollox East Goods

Springburn Jn.

Robroyston Colliery

Burmulloch Jn.

Milton Jn.

Springburn

NBL Atlas Wks.

St. Rollox
loco shed   Balornock Jn.

Cowlairs
Works

NBL
Hydepark Wks.   Barnhill Jn.
Sighthill Jn.   Barnhill
Germiston Jns.
Low.

Craighall Goods   Sighthill
East Jn.

Forth & Clyde Canal   Tennants
Wks.   2   Sighthill Gds.   High

Port Dundas Branch   b   Blackhill Jn.

Pinkston Power
Station   Provan Gas Works   Blochairn
Jn.

d   e   St. Rollox
Works   Blochairn
Ironworks   Monkland Canal

Buchanan Street   Garngad   Gds.

Townhead

Gds.   Monkland Canal

Queen Street   Gds.

Alexandra Parade   Kennyhill Goods

Haghill Jn.
To Bellgrove   To Carntyne   To Dalmarnock
Gds.

Below. Despite its unprepossessing nature, Buchanan Street was the station for several important cities and some of the loveliest parts of Scotland. There were stopping trains to Stirling, Perth and Alloa, the Aberdeen and Dundee expresses, and services to Callander and Oban. Places on the destination board included Dunblane, Balquhidder, Gleneagles and Crieff. Most trains were formed of modern stock and particularly in LMS years many had restaurant cars. There was no call for an extensive local and suburban timetable and most passengers were business travellers or long distance season ticket holders. With about 30 trains each way a day there tended to be bursts of activity at critical times, punctuated by long periods of quiet. There was also an upsurge of traffic at holiday times with duplicate, relief and divided trains being run. A few days before it was dieselised, the 13.15 to Dundee West left Buchanan Street behind Standard class 5 4–6–0 No.73157 on 29th October 1965. Note the peculiar suspended signals with the miniature arms above them for shunting movements.

Northern Approaches

Carriage shed at Townhead.

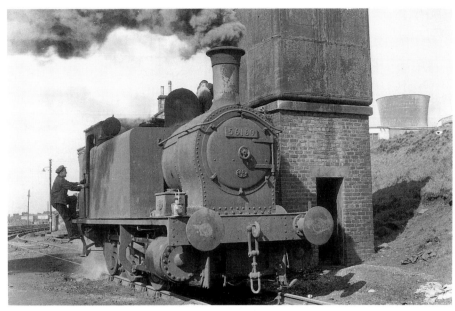

Besides having a remote and elevated location beyond the city limits, the Garnkirk terminus at Townhead was surrounded by industrial premises including the malodorous Tennants chemical works. It was the only passenger station in Glasgow for ten years and had a steady flow of customers between 1831 and 1849, but goods traffic was always more at home here. Living up to this image admirably, very scruffy McIntosh 0–6–0 tank No.56169 from St. Rollox shed took water at Townhead on 16th April 1960. Peeping above the engine is the simple sandstone carriage shed and dwelling house once thought of as an original G & G building but most likely dating from the 1840s. To the right is one of the cooling towers of the huge Pinkston Power Station built by Glasgow Corporation in 1901 for the electrification of the tramways. Later it supplied power for the Underground and trolleybuses but was handed over to the South of Scotland Electricity Board in 1958 and has now been demolished. There was traffic on the branch for a structural engineering works, oil depot, scrap yard and distillery besides the power station and chemical factory. St. Rollox West, as Townhead had become, ceased to accept public goods traffic in July 1968 and the remaining private sidings closed shortly afterwards. By this time an 0–4–0 diesel shunter had been the motive power for some time. The site is now obliterated by the M8 motorway.

Much of the Monklands plateau north east of Glasgow is around 300ft above sea level and from its western extremity at Balornock just over 2 miles from the city centre the land drops sharply down to the Clyde. This was the topography faced by the early lines into Glasgow's two main line termini on the north side – Buchanan Street and Queen Street. As a result both approaches featured significant inclines and fairly long tunnels, in order to lose height. The stations themselves were built as rudimentary timber sheds, although Queen Street was described rather ludicrously as 'an almost fairy palace' in an early guide book. There were no kind words at all about Buchanan Street and as magnificent railway buildings appeared elsewhere in Britain both termini were frequently condemned as a disgrace to the city. Buchanan Street was enlarged over the years but remained primitive and even when the LMS rebuilt it in the early 1930s it was still a poor show for Glasgow's gateway to the Highlands, Tayside and the Grampian coast. Reconstruction of Queen Street during 1879 resulted in the superb glazed roof which can still be appreciated today, but this airy arch has always disguised the immense difficulties in working traffic at this particular Glasgow station. The lines serving Buchanan Street and Queen Street were both tremendous Scottish railway pioneers in their own way, although both put the second city of the empire second in their titles. The Garnkirk & Glasgow Railway, from which the tracks to Buchanan Street eventually sprang, opened in 1831. It ran from Gartsherrie near Coatbridge – on the even earlier Monkland & Kirkintilloch Railway – to Townhead next to Tennant's factory at St. Rollox. The idea was to bring coal to the city in general and the chemical works in particular, but steam locomotives were used from the outset and there was a regular passenger service. The Edinburgh & Glasgow Railway opened in 1842 as the first massively engineered major trunk route in Scotland. It completely revolutionised transport between the two cities, which over the centuries had ranged from a man on foot carrying the post to a combined rail and canal journey via the Garnkirk line. Ironically this almost level, high speed inter-city route entered Glasgow by means of Cowlairs bank – probably the most awkward

and operationally expensive incline on any main line in Britain. Both the G & G and E & G lines still carry passenger services. Buchanan Street station however has been closed and totally obliterated whilst Queen Street welcomes passengers to class 158 diesel units, the latest generation in over 150 years of Edinburgh expresses.

BUCHANAN STREET

The 4ft. 6in. gauge Garnkirk & Glasgow Railway opened quietly during May 1831 for minerals and carried its first passengers on 1st June. However, a spectacular official opening ceremony was staged by the proprietors for publicity purposes on 27th September 1831 when the two English – built Stephenson locomotives showed what they could do and crowds cheered them on. From Gartsherrie the 8 mile line headed vaguely north westwards across the Monklands plateau through Gartcosh, assumed a westerly course at the obscure hamlet of Garnkirk which inspired the company's name, then turned south west towards Glasgow at Robroyston. Engineering requirements had been light this far, but just

short of St. Rollox a massive embankment was required at Germiston and when the City of Glasgow Union line pierced it 40 years later a short tunnel rather than a bridge was needed. Townhead terminus was at Glebe Street just west of Springburn Road and adjacent to the Monkland Canal. Coal was by far the most important traffic and there were extensive facilities for transferring it to barges, road carts and Tennant's works. The yard presented a busy scene, but from the passenger's point of view it was inconvenient for the city and had extremely primitive facilities. So it is quite remarkable that Townhead handled Anglo–Scottish traffic from the completion of the Caledonian main line on 15th February 1848 to the opening of the Clydesdale Junction Railway, giving access to South Side station on 1st June 1849 (see Southern Approaches). The G & G had extended its tracks south from Gartsherrie to Coatbridge in 1844 and rechristened itself the Glasgow, Garnkirk & Coatbridge. Here it joined the Wishaw & Coltness, another local Monklands line. Both were taken over by the budding Caledonian in 1847 and regauged to 4ft. 8½in. Trains from Carlisle

After World War 2 Buchanan Street was virtually monopolized by St. Rollox and Perth ex–LMS class 5s, which were later joined by Standard class 5s. But just as the erstwhile mecca at Queen Street was losing its fascination, Buchanan Street became the centre of interest with the introduction of Gresley A4 Pacifics on the 3 hour Aberdeen trains in June 1962. They could also be seen on Dundee West services and postal workings. With its gorgeous chime whistle echoing round the station, 60009 UNION OF SOUTH AFRICA set off for Aberdeen with the 5.30 pm 'St. Mungo' on 31st August 1962. On the left Standard class 5 No.73147 was ready with the 5.35 pm to Dunblane and in the centre ex–LMS class 5 No.45153 waited with the 6.5 pm to Oban. The A4s finished in September 1966. Buchanan Street goods, opened in January 1850 and the largest depot in Scotland until 1907, finally closed on 6th August 1962. The passenger station followed on 7th November 1966. Its cramped sloping concourse, woebegone buffet and appalling toilets which had greeted travellers for decades were immediately swept away along with the rest of the terminus. Buchanan bus station, an extension of Cowcaddens Road, Scotrail House and the Glasgow Caledonian University (presumably 'Caley' for short!) now occupy the site.

joined the Coltness line at Garriongill Junction just south of Wishaw.

Even the Garnkirk company had planned a passenger terminus nearer the city centre and construction work on a proposed rope–worked incline had already started when the Caledonian took over. They had different ideas and took a branch off the Garnkirk line at Milton Junction well short of Townhead. It descended steadily for 2 miles, largely at 1 in 80, and included a 400 yard tunnel under Port Dundas, the canal, and part of the Tennants complex. In fact the eastern approach cutting to the tunnel was carved out of a huge mass of evil smelling chemical waste on the edge of the works. The new terminus was at the northern end of Buchanan Street where it joined Port Dundas Road, Cowcaddens Street and West Nile Street and services began on 1st November 1849. In terms of accessibility it was a vast improvement on Townhead but financial constraints meant that no attempt was made to create a prestigious station. In fact the architecture and facilities were abysmal. Originally Buchanan Street had just two platforms, partly sheltered by broad low–pitched timber roofs supported on wooden columns, and a dismal single storey block containing essential offices. English traffic was immediately transferred from South Side and there were through trains to Edinburgh as well as local Monklands services. The Caledonian invited designs for a new station in 1857 but despite many entries nothing was done.

At least the following decade saw some extensions and improvements enabling Caley services from Stirling, Perth and Aberdeen to use the station – previously they had been handled at Queen Street. The transfer of Edinburgh and English traffic to the new Central station on 1st September 1879 quashed any incentive for further improvements however. When the LMS acquired Buchanan Street in 1923 it presented three wooden gable ends to the street, the centre one being slightly larger. Each had a plain round–headed window, the right hand one had a small clock, and there was a feeble canopy supported on six slender columns. The whole sorry structure was replaced in 1932. Fortunately the rambling Lanarkshire & Ayrshire station at Ardrossan North had just closed and its platform canopies were redeployed at Buchanan Street. The frontage and concourse were provided with a new steel framed structure faced in timber. With its severely angular proportions, mock columns, pronounced cornice and small tower, the building had classical pretensions along with lots of others dating from the 1930s, but its overall impact was weak. As a railway terminus it would have been more at home in a Borders market town.

Just over half way up the incline out of Buchanan Street the Caledonian established a new locomotive, carriage and wagon works at St. Rollox in 1882. Eventually it occupied 24

acres including 13 acres under cover, employed 3000 men, and dealt with most of the company's rolling stock repairs as well as new construction. At its height the plant had the capacity to build 50 locomotives, 100 coaches and 3000 wagons a year besides its regular refurbishment programme. The whole process of turning basic materials into railway equipment took place here. Logs arrived at the sawmill and drying yard, eventually emerging as carriage bodywork or fine interior detailing. Castings were made in the foundry and metal was processed by steam hammers, hydraulic presses and hot saws. There was a huge variety of machines including those for drilling, shearing, punching, milling, grinding and polishing as well as some for making bolts and rivets. Tinsmiths, coppersmiths, trimmers and painters had their own workshops. Although small by comparison, the design office where a dozen or so draughtsmen worked was vitally important and from 1895 it produced the elegant Caley locos inspired by J.F. McIntosh. After grouping St. Rollox concentrated on overhauling engines from LMS Scottish sheds and this continued after nationalisation. Towards the end of steam the Glasgow plant also dealt with a few English locos, including Brighton–designed Standard 4MT 4–6–0s in the 75000 series – a type never allocated north of the border. During 1965 a green–liveried example even appeared on a Paisley Canal line running–in turn.

14

Immediately beyond Buchanan Street the railway passed under Dobbies Loan which had brick arches over the passenger lines and a big lattice girder bridge across the goods yard approach. The large fan of rails then converged to form just two tracks through the tunnel. Beyond it lay the fetid chemical cutting, a deep bridge under Springburn Road, then the large but basic wayside station at St. Rollox opened on 1st August 1883. Here, on 2nd September 1954, Standard class 5 No 73006 was making steady progress up the incline with its rake of 'blood & custard' coaches forming the 5.0 pm 'Saint Mungo' to Aberdeen. It was climbing unassisted – banking engines were occasionally used at Buchanan Street on heavy holiday trains, but not on a regular basis. The 'Saint Mungo' was one of the 3 hour trains introduced by the LMS in 1938 but discontinued during the war. Although the name was revived in 1949 the 3 hour schedule was not reinstated until 1962, and both train and title were lost with the closure of Buchanan Street. Tenements and a chapel at the corner of Fountainwell Road and Springburn Road formed a perfectly composed backdrop while class N15 0–6–2 tank No.69197 shunted one of the more obscure corners of the ex–North British Sighthill goods yard with one of the footplate crew casting an admiring glance towards the Aberdeen express. St. Rollox station closed on 5th November 1962 and the site is now derelict, but St. Rollox Works high up to the left and out of view was still repairing diesel locomotives thirty years later. Sighthill depot closed suddenly on 5th October 1981 when there were still up to 14 trip workings a day from the yard.

Robroyston Yard stood on the north side of the main line 3 ½ miles out of Buchanan Street and was used for general marshalling purposes. Seen from Bogside Road bridge on 29th April 1961, recently outshopped WD 2–8–0 No.90553 shunted the yard as Type 2 diesels Nos.D6117 and D6136 passed with the 12 noon service from Buchanan Street to Oban. The fireman observed the passing train, but this time most likely out of sympathy rather than admiration. These machines were the sad swansong of Glasgow's mighty North British Locomotive Company and suffered repeated failures following their introduction on services to the Argyllshire coast in January 1961. They were soon ousted by the more reliable 'Birmingham Sulzers' (later class 27) although re–engined examples occasionally appeared in the West Highlands as late as 1969. Robroyston yard closed in 1967, by which time there was no trace of the little chalet–style passenger station nearby, abandoned in 1956. St. Rollox loco shed was 1 ½ miles away in the distance. It never had an allocation of main line diesels and closed at the same time as Buchanan Street.

QUEEN STREET

A weekly stagecoach between Glasgow and Edinburgh was introduced as early 1678, but it failed to pay and soon stopped running. Another attempt was made in 1749 and this time the service prospered to the extent that there were ten return journeys a week by the 1830s and journey times were down to about four hours. With the completion of the Union Canal from Falkirk to Edinburgh in 1822 through boat journeys via the Forth & Clyde Canal were also on offer if travellers had most of the day to spare. No doubt spurred on by the exciting prospects of the Stockton & Darlington Railway, an enterprising group proposed a line between Leith Docks and Broomielaw Quay in Glasgow during 1825 but the scheme was smothered by the all–powerful canal proprietors. With the tide of opinion moving towards railways, an Act was finally obtained for a line from Edinburgh Haymarket to Glasgow Queen Street in July 1838 and the Edinburgh & Glasgow Railway was about to begin its long career. There was the inevitable opposition from certain landowners and some bad weather to contend with during construction, but after a huge banquet and general rejoicing at Queen Street two days previously, the line was opened to passenger traffic on 21st February 1842.

The E & G was built as a superb high speed line with massive engineering works to maintain its almost level course across the Forth–Clyde watershed. For 15 miles the approach from Falkirk remained just below the 250 foot contour and when Croy Hill got in the way a deep rock cutting was gouged through it for

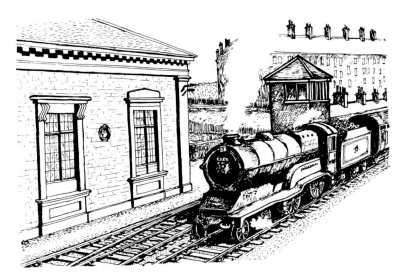

Classical features adorned the Edinburgh & Glasgow Railway Incline Engine House at the top of Cowlairs Bank.

nearly 2000 yards. From Croy to Cowlairs the tracks descended mainly at a barely noticeable 1 in 1285 although a viaduct at Lenzie and a long cutting at Bishopbriggs were necessary to achieve this. At Cowlairs, 200 feet above sea level, the tracks veered sharply right and plummeted for 1 ¼ miles, firstly at 1 in 41, then 1 in 43, and finally 1 in 51 for a short stretch before levelling out at Queen Street a mere 50ft above the tidal Clyde. Almost exactly half of the descent was in Cowlairs tunnel. Originally a gentler gradient to a high level

terminus on ground above the eventual tunnel was proposed, but the Forth & Clyde Canal objected to a bridge over their Port Dundas branch and forced the railway underground. A couple of wide shafts or 'eyes' through solid sandstone ventilated the lower part of the tunnel, but the trickiest engineering came a few years later, in the upper half, when the Caledonian's Buchanan Street extension was being built. Having just emerged from its own tunnel, the newer line was only a few feet above the crown of the E & G bore and special brac-

On 3rd October 1955 the customary smoke haze at Queen Street was exacerbated by a damp Glasgow afternoon heralding the onset of winter. Class D11/2 4–4–0 No.62673 EVAN DHU, one of the LNER engines based on Great Central Railway 'Large Directors' and built specially for service in Scotland, waited with the 5.6 pm relief to Thornton Junction. It was Fife Autumn Holiday, thus the need for this additional Monday evening service. The lattice girders support Cathedral Street which was at first above the tunnel entrance, thus emphasising the cramped nature of the original station. Opening up the approach put the tunnel mouth further back beyond an even higher bridge which carried Holmhead Street. Well off to the left was Queen Street goods depot, also facing George Square, and it was served by 'lifts' up and down the incline which had to fit in with the intense passenger service. Loadings were limited to 14 wagons which had to have sufficient brakes pinned down during the descent and a 20 ton brake van at the rear when ascending. Even by the 1930s Queen Street goods was concerned mainly with just potatoes and beer and this remained the case until closure on 6th January 1964. Its site is now occupied by a car park and taxi rank.

ing was necessary in the cutting to protect the underground arch. At first Cowlairs tunnel was lit by over 40 gas lamps in big lanterns, and seven weeks before the line opened the enterprising E & G allowed the public to inspect it for a small charge.

Although the steam locomotive had proved itself by the early 1840s it was still a relatively feeble machine compared with those built a couple of decades later. Obviously a gradient of 1 in 41 would cause severe difficulties even with lightweight trains and for nearly 70 years Cowlairs incline was worked by a cumbersome and costly alternative. At the top of the bank stood a stone building housing 80 hp high pressure stationary steam engines with 36 inch diameter and 6ft. stroke cylinders. By means

of a continuous hemp rope guided by pulleys between the rails, departing trains were hauled out of Queen Street complete with their locos. In the opposite direction the rope was not used. Instead, specially constructed brake vehicles (heavy 4-wheel open metal trucks with prominent horizontal brake wheels on columns) controlled the descent. They were also placed at the rear of ascending trains in case of mishaps with the rope. Unfortunately Glasgow's damp weather affected the hemp and the resultant slipping reduced progress to a virtual standstill on several occasions. In an attempt to rectify this situation, the first job given to newly established Cowlairs Works was an order for two powerful locomotives for banking duties. They appeared in 1844 and

did their job – but played havoc with the track, ruptured the tunnel lining despite iron plates installed to deflect the exhaust, and caused vibrations sufficient to make the Forth & Clyde Canal leak. The engines were dispatched to Monklands coalfield duties in 1848 and cable operation resumed using a much heftier 5 inch circumference wire weighing 25 tons.

Originally Queen Street station was a pitifully cramped affair cowering in an old sandstone quarry below Dundas Street. It was covered by a steeply pitched roof supported on two rows of 48 iron columns and finished off with crude gable ends consisting of horizontal planks. The platforms extended as far as the tunnel mouth, yet passengers still had to venture inside it to reach the front carriages of

Queen's Street's splendid new roof with its fan-shaped end screens extended for 450ft. from the concourse a few yards from George Square to within a couple of feet of the Cathedral Street viaduct. Its gentle curve was 250ft. wide, 80ft. above track level in the centre, and was supported either side by rows of bulky 24ft. cast iron columns with flamboyant floral capitals.

The North British built several big 0–6–2 tanks for pushing trains up Cowlairs bank after the end of rope working. On 3rd April 1961 N15 No.69181 stood at the buffers blowing off steam as it waited to bank a train out of platform 2. One of the dignified roof support columns and the less elegant 1950s ticket office facade formed the background. A wire from the coupling passed over the little pulley on the smokebox to a lever in the cab and at Cowlairs this was pulled, thus lifting the link with the last coach. Occasionally this primitive system failed to work and there was much frantic whistling from the banker as the train began to accelerate.

Cowlairs incline was a busy and extremely noisy stretch of track where the demonic energy of the steam engine was seen at its best, especially on a bright cold winter day. B1 No.61134 heading the 10.50 am 'Queen of Scots' Pullman hammered up the last few yards of the bank at 25–30 mph on 1st March 1954 with an N15 working just as hard at the rear. The 'Queen of Scots' from Glasgow Queen Street to London King's Cross via Edinburgh Waverley commenced in 1928, was withdrawn from 1939 to 1948 because of the war, and finally ceased running in 1964. In this view from near Keppochhill Road the tenements of Coxhill Street and the bridge to Sighthill Cemetery are in the middle distance. The track on the right was the Port Dundas East branch which curved away behind Coxhill Street to serve Pinkston Power Station and a goods depot on Craighall Road. It closed to public goods traffic on 31st March 1969 and finally on 19th March 1979, having latterly just served a coal merchant. With the redevelopment of Sighthill a number of tower blocks reared above Cowlairs bank and unfortunately fostered a generation which turned this stretch of line into one of the worst in Britain for stone throwing.

At the top of the incline an abrupt curve took the tracks through Cowlairs station which was rebuilt by the North British with an island platform and characteristically dull buildings when rope working was abandoned. The winding house then became an electrical switch room for nearby Cowlairs Works and it was still there in the 1950s, overlooked by the houses of Morrin Street in the background. Part of the works can be seen on the right. An hourly service was operated from Glasgow Queen Street to Edinburgh Waverley and on 21st October 1955 Peppercorn A2 Pacific No.60530 SAYAJIRAO had finished climbing out of the Clyde valley and was ready to build up speed with the 12 noon express. The 4–6–2s shared these duties with V2 2–6–2s, B1 4–6–0s and D11 4–4–0s in early BR years. Although Cowlairs was already grimy and unkempt, the splendid clock was not only working but showing the right time. The station closed to passengers on 7th September 1964 and goods facilities were withdrawn in April 1966.

Cowlairs Works opened shortly after the Edinburgh & Glasgow Railway and eventually developed into a complex similar to St. Rollox half a mile away across Sighthill Cemetery. On 16th August 1958 four locomotives were being overhauled in the erecting shop, from left to right K2 2–6–0 No.61766, J39 0–6–0 No.64875, K3 2–6–0 No.61851 and WD 2–8–0 No.90762. At the time the whole range of engines based at former LNER sheds in the Scottish Region were repaired at Cowlairs, except Pacifics and V2 2–6–2s which were sent south of the border. On the other hand locos from certain English sheds were dispatched to Glasgow for attention – in fact the last engine to pass through Cowlairs was a K1 2–6–0 from the North Eastern Region. The works closed in 1966, never having dealt with diesels, and the site is now occupied by an industrial estate.

Having cleared Cowlairs station and left its banker behind, A3 Pacific No.60094 COLORADO took advantage of the billiard table gradients of the E & G to build up speed with the 4 pm 'North Briton' from Glasgow Queen Street to Leeds Central on 25th September 1954. This particular Anglo–Scottish train began running as long ago as 1910 but was not named until early BR days. By 1970 the service had been cut back to Edinburgh and the title dropped. The 1950s were still days of plenty and there was also a 4 pm from Glasgow St. Enoch to Leeds City via the Settle & Carlisle route which for those in a hurry was 20 minutes quicker. Eastfield shed with a D11 4–4–0 dominating a line of J83 0–6–0 tanks was in the background and the ex–Caledonian freight line from Dalmarnock to Possil ran across the long plate girder viaduct in the middle distance.

long trains. A monumental Propylaeum similar to that just erected 350 miles away in Euston Square, London, was envisaged at first. However the entrance facing George Square materialised as an uninspiring arch between West George Street Chapel, commonly known as Wardlaw's Kirk, and a nondescript house. At first the 'fairy palace' had just four departures for Edinburgh Haymarket at 7 am, 11 am, 3 pm and 5 pm, the fastest taking 135 minutes. Whilst a few passengers went first class and enjoyed upholstered seats, arm rests and glazed windows in best stagecoach tradition, the larger ranks of second class travellers were treated to wooden benches and a lot of fresh air through the open sides, but the poor souls in third class had to stand in open trucks and avoid the sparks. Demand was phenomenal however and the service was soon doubled. By 1846 the E & G was carrying three times the number of people expected by the promoters and four years later the company needed 58 locomotives and 216 coaches to cope with its passenger traffic.

The Edinburgh & Glasgow Railway was absorbed by the North British on 1st August 1865. Working the terminus and incline became increasingly difficult with the relentless increase in traffic and early in 1877 local magistrates condemned Queen Street as the most inconvenient and dangerous station in Glasgow. Despite its frugal policies the North British was shamed into spending some money on its property in the city. An extensive programme begun in late 1877 involved the opening up of the lower end of Cowlairs tunnel, thus widening the station approach and allowing six platforms to be built, whilst at the same time a fine overall glass roof was erected. Further relief came in 1886 with the opening of Queen Street Low Level which absorbed most of the rapidly growing suburban traffic. It took the form of four lengthy through platforms underneath and at right angles to the main line station (see North British Suburban chapter). By the early 1900s the terminus was handling Aberdeen and Dundee expresses together with 20 or so Edinburghs, some with through coaches to London King's Cross. There were also West Highland services to Fort William and Mallaig, trains to Larbert, Stirling, Perth and the Fife Coast, and locals to lesser known places such as Lennoxtown, Aberfoyle, Kilsyth and Bonnybridge. Over 38,000 passengers were being dealt with on summer weekdays and this rose to 50,000 on Glasgow Spring Holiday. With a compulsory 7 minutes between departures and a large annual bill for operation and maintenance, Cowlairs Incline was becoming an increasing source of irritation however. Electrification was suggested but by August 1909 all trains were ascending by steam traction alone, albeit with the help of banking engines.

In the 1950s many passengers saw Queen Street station as a dismal dirty place to begin a journey, but from the enthusiast's point of view it was fascinating. It was perhaps at its most atmospheric on a gloomy winter day when a particularly dense knot of smoke masked the cavernous tunnel entrance, endless shunting movements took place in a kind of organised chaos – banking engines simmered under the arched roof and ear–piercing jets of steam from safety valves occasionally obliter-

ated the general hub–bub. The following observations are from the notebook of a young W.A.C. Smith who joined a little gathering of spotters around the fogman's brazier at the end of platform 5 one November afternoon in 1950...

On entering the station, Peppercorn A1 No.60152 (in LNER apple green and not yet named HOLYROOD) was noted at platform 2, the main arrival platform, with the 8.55 am 'North Briton' from Leeds, its coaches now forming the 4.0 pm return working. Meanwhile N15 banker No.69183 was in place at platform 5 with the 3.46 pm to Mallaig. Instead of the expected pair of K2 moguls, Eastfield shed had turned out D34 4–4–0s Nos.62474 GLEN CROE and 62498 GLEN MOIDART for this train which departed 3 minutes late and flaunted express passenger headlamps evoking memories of earlier years. Previously, four locos had come down the incline coupled together and were identified through the swirling fog as A2 60534 IRISH ELEGANCE, D11 4–4–0 62676 JONATHAN OLDBUCK, B1 4–6–0 No.61403 and D49 4–4–0 No.62708 ARGYLLSHIRE. The B1, allocated to Kittybrewster and ex–Cowlairs Works, went on to the 'Fife Coast Express' at platform 1 (departing at 4.7 pm for St. Andrews and frequently – though not on this occasion – sporting an articulated set from the pre-war 'Silver Jubilee'). The A2 backed on to

an extra coach for the 'North Briton' which had been placed in platform 4 ahead of the 4.19 pm for Grangemouth and N15 No.9138 (not yet renumbered by BR) coupled on as pilot. After more empty stock had come down the tunnel the two engines backed on to the main part of the train, now consisting of 12 vehicles. The 'North Briton' departed 7 minutes late banked by the A1 slipping violently, followed by the 'Fife Coast Express'. The 3.0 pm from Edinburgh then arrived in platform 3 at 4.14 pm – 10 minutes late behind B1 61244 STRANG STEEL. After the D49 had left on the 4.13 pm to Thornton Junction, station pilot J83 0–6–0 tank No.68479 placed the 11 Edinburgh coaches in platform 2 (where banker 69183 was already in position) to form the 5.0 pm departure for the capital. The released B1 then went to platform 4 and was attached in front of the D11 on the 4.19 pm to Grangemouth for the climb to Cowlairs. The train consisted of four non–corridor coaches and got away at 4.28 pm. Further departures were the 4.40 pm to Perth via Alloa with D34 No.62470 GLEN ROY and the 4.48 pm to Kilsyth with No.62477 GLEN DOCHART, while green B1 61072 came in with the 1.45 pm from Dundee Tay Bridge due 4.39 pm but 10 minutes late. A surprising sight was the 5.0 pm to Edinburgh going out hauled by N15 No.69188 with 69183 banking, the train engine taking over at Cowlairs.∎

Eastfield depot, the largest on the North British system, opened in September 1904 and occupied a substantial area on the east side of the main line half a mile beyond Cowlairs station. It had its share of Edinburgh, West Highland and Fife passenger turns together with the occasional Dundee and Perth services and there were also numerous freight duties including shunting Cadder Yard. On 12th September 1962 B1s Nos.61396 and 61398 simmered in front of Eastfield's mighty coaling tower as J37 No.64623 took on water. Steam traction finished in 1966 but the depot survived until October 1992.

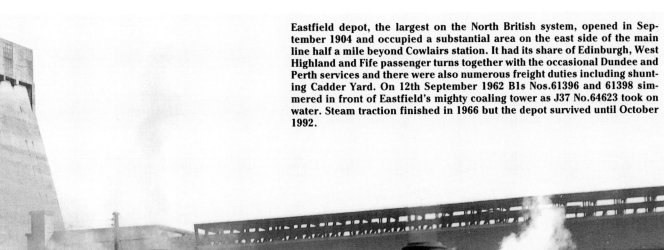

Cadder Yard opened in October 1901 to relieve chronic congestion at Sighthill, College and Queen Street goods depots. On 27th July 1960 K2 2–6–0 No.61788 LOCH RANNOCH left Cadder with a modest freight. By this time the survivors of the thirty ex–Great Northern Railway Moguls transferred to Scotland (fourteen in 1925, six in 1932 and ten in 1951) were worn out and employed on menial duties after many years pounding the West Highland line. 61788 was withdrawn in June 1961 and Cadder Yard finally closed during the 1970s after a long decline.

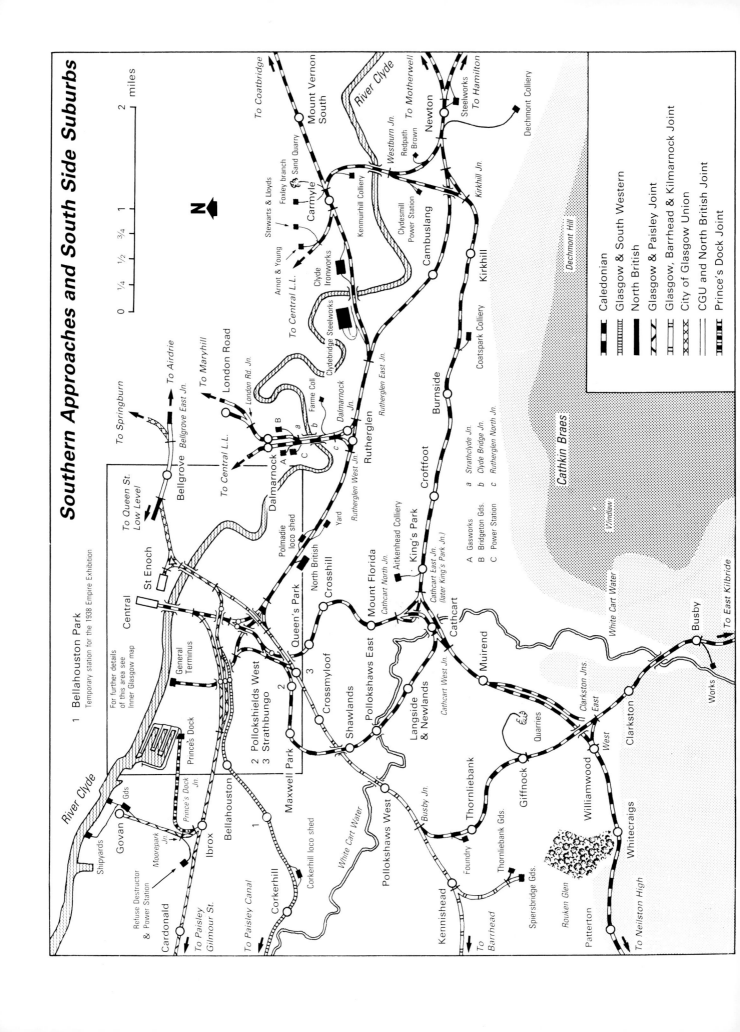

Southern Approaches and South Side Suburbs

Southern Approaches

Queen Street and Buchanan Street stations had fairly straightforward origins and were established early. In marked contrast the sequence of events leading to the opening of St. Enoch and Central thirty years later was far more complex. Although the three southern approaches were there by the late 1840s they terminated south of the Clyde and dogged resistance to a railway bridge across the river blocked further progress until circumstances dictated that something had to be done. The Paisley, Barrhead and Rutherglen routes were busy enough with a mixture of local passenger and mineral trains, and the last one was even used by passengers from England during 1849. However, once the Clyde had been spanned all of them became important main lines carrying a variety of traffic including Anglo–Scottish expresses and Irish boat trains.

The rails from Ayr and Greenock via Paisley arrived first and trains began to use Bridge Street station on the south side of the Clyde opposite the Broomielaw in 1840. A wide area was opened up and several important towns were served, virtually guaranteeing success. Next came the Barrhead line which opened in 1848 and terminated at South Side station a

good mile from the city centre. On the ground it was a local line, but on the map it was a finger pointing towards Kilmarnock. The Rutherglen route opened in 1849 as a branch from the Caledonian at Motherwell direct to Glasgow. It also went to South Side and shared the disadvantages of that terminus for thirty years.

Pressure mounted for a freight link between the north and south side lines as well as a central passenger station accessible from the southern approaches. A railway bridge across the Clyde actually in Glasgow had become a necessity and from 1865 to 1879 a lot of money was spent providing two of them. The City of Glasgow Union ran from the Paisley line just short of Bridge Street, crossed the river west of Glasgow Green and forged a link with the North British near High Street. On the way it thrust out a spur towards St. Enoch Square and built Glasgow's first grand terminus. The Caledonian response was an extension from Bridge Street across the Clyde to another city terminus on Gordon Street. Thus 'Glasgow Central' opened in 1879 together with connections to the Barrhead and Rutherglen lines, but it was another 25 years before Central was metamorphosed into the

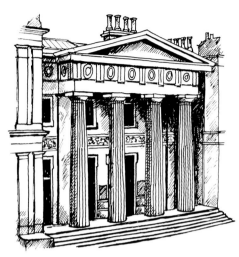

The original classical facade to Bridge Street station.

Bridge Street was Glasgow's first substantial station and despite having closed over fifty years earlier, the main buildings were still visible from the 12.50 pm Glasgow Central to Gourock on 30th December 1958. Fairburn 2–6–4T No.42244 was on empty stock and the 12.54 pm from Central to Kirkhill was about to pass a light engine in the murky distance. On 6th April 1841 the makeshift wooden affair at Bridge Street was replaced by a permanent structure consisting of four tracks, two platforms and twin train sheds braced by thin metal ties and supported on columns. It stood on arches and the building rising from street level featured a monumental Grecian portico in cream stone. The extension to Central involved widening the viaduct and a complete rebuild at rail level. By 1879 there were two through tracks with four bays for Caledonian and G & SW locals and this time the overall roof was carried on deep lattice girders spanning the whole station. Withdrawal of the remaining G & SW trains in 1892 and the subsequent enlargement of Central rendered Bridge Street obsolete and it closed on 1st March 1905. The original classical terminus building can be seen above the first coach of the empty stock. It was demolished in 1971, but the huge rambling Queen Anne style extension of 1888 behind the engine still survives.

magnificent station still in use today.

GLASGOW AND PAISLEY

Paisley grew rapidly in the early 1800s as a result of its flourishing textile industry and the population of coastal towns such as Ayr and Greenock were also increasing. The Glasgow, Paisley & Ardrossan Canal which opened between Port Eglinton on the south side of Glasgow and Paisley in 1813 proved very useful, but by the late 1820s there was already talk of a railway from Glasgow to Paisley. In 1836 groups were set up to build lines from both Ayr and Greenock to the city. A certain amount of jostling took place over their respective approaches to Glasgow, but common sense prevailed and the Acts which authorised the Glasgow, Paisley, Kilmarnock & Ayr and Glasgow, Paisley & Greenock on 15th July 1837 also stipulated a jointly–owned section, from Paisley towards Glasgow.

The Glasgow & Paisley Joint line opened on 14th July 1840, although the permanent terminus at Bridge Street was not ready for another nine months. It was double track and mainly pursued an easy course across flat farmland with the only engineering works of note being a viaduct on the approach to Bridge Street and a short tunnel – later opened out to a cutting – at Arkleston near Paisley. Trains lurched along unconsolidated track and 3rd class passengers swayed about in open wagons without seats during that first summer, but the line was a resounding success. No less than 53,000 people (equivalent to a quarter of Glasgow's population at the time) travelled on it during the first month alone and new 4–wheel carriages and 2–2–2 engines were set to work immediately they were delivered.

Almost as soon as it opened the GPK & A advertised itself as the fastest route from Glasgow to London, the journey involving a new steamer service between Ardrossan and Liverpool. This proved unpopular and was one of the few failures of the Paisley route. Instead the line prospered on local business, although eventually boats began to play an important role as the highly competitive Clyde Coast residential and holiday traffic developed. On 28th October 1850 the GPK & A became one of the two founder members of the Glasgow & South Western and on 9th July 1847 the GP & G was absorbed by the Caledonian. Consequently the Paisley – Bridge Street section became a joint G&SW/Caledonian operation. The system remains as important as ever and electrification of the Greenock route took place on 5th June 1967, followed by the Ayr line on 29th September 1986.

Govan is one of the oldest ecclesiastical sites in Scotland but during the 19th century its name became synonymous with shipbuilding and over the years its yards launched many famous liners. A branch opened from Ibrox on the Paisley Joint line on 1st May 1868 and passenger trains to Bridge Street followed on 2nd December. This was one of the earliest suburban services in the city and became quite intensive after the City of Glasgow Union opened. It also gained coverage in the national press when the line became the first in the country to surrender to trams. An earlier victim of competition was the Ardrossan Canal which had valiantly fought the Glasgow & Paisley Joint line on 1st May 1868 and passenger trains to Bridge Street followed on 2nd December. This was one of the earliest suburban services in the city and became quite intensive after the City of Glasgow Union opened. It also gained coverage in the national press when the line became the first in the country to surrender to trams. An earlier victim of competition was the Ardrossan Canal which had valiantly fought the Glasgow & Paisley Joint with cheap rates but eventually sold out to the G & SW. It was promptly converted into a rather tortuous but independent second route to Paisley – the Canal line, opened on 1st July 1885. The Canal line missed its centenary as a passenger route by virtue of an appalling saga, which involved the withdrawal of services in 1983, despite vehement opposition, and their costly but very popular reinstatement 7½ years later.

The Glasgow & Paisley Joint, City of Glasgow Union and Paisley Canal line came together at Shields Road just under a mile out of Bridge Street. Each line had its own station, virtually side by side, and the General Terminus branch passed below all three of them. Connections between the various routes made this one of the most complex railway locations in Britain. Tram No 13 bound for Mount Florida passed the City Union's intricate wooden frontage at Shields Road about noon on Christmas Day 1957. At the time there was still a normal suburban train service in Glasgow at Christmas, although from 1958 certain services were shut down as was already the case at New Year. During the 1950s December 25th was a school, shop and office holiday in Glasgow but a normal working day for factories and heavy industry. There were even postal deliveries! The last BR trains anywhere on Christmas Day ran in the city in 1982. In the background at the corner of Shields Road and Scotland Street is Kinning Park church, one of 'Greek' Thomson's noble edifices. Unfortunately this particular one was demolished about 1960.

Sparkling Haymarket A1 Pacific No.60152 HOLYROOD propelled the early morning Edinburgh Waverley – Glasgow Salkeld Street parcels train through the Paisley Joint platforms at Shields Road, originally Pollokshields station, on 21st September 1963. This working, which was usually a diesel turn at the time, had come in over the City of Glasgow Union and had reversed on to the Paisley Joint line west of Shields Road. Salkeld Street parcels depot had opened at the former G & SW Eglinton Street goods station on 6th July 1959.

The City Union booking office at Shields Road presented a less attractive aspect to the platforms as was apparent on 16th May 1960 when Hughes 'Crab' 2–6–0 No.42739 paused in evening sunshine with the 6.25 pm St. Enoch – Kilmarnock via Dalry. These platforms opened on 1st June 1871 when G & SW 'bus trains' to Bellgrove commenced. Pollokshields station on the Glasgow & Paisley Joint was immediately to the left, its westbound track using the other side of the CGU platform. There was no road frontage. Shields station on the Canal line opened on 1st July 1885 and is prominent on the right. Originally it had delicate iron cresting along the roof and even a weather vane on a pole, but by 1960 these had been removed. On 1st April 1925 the LMS amalgamated these three stations as Shields Road and a diminishing number of passengers used the sprawl of platforms until closure on 14th February 1966. The signals to the right of the engine controlled low level lines and the General Terminus branch was below the low wall on the left.

A good impression of the very complex layout at Shields Road could be gained from a walkway at the side of the former City Union booking office, as in this 4th July 1958 view. Shields station on the Canal line was at the top of the bank to the left, whilst Shields Road and Pollokshields on the St. Enoch and Central routes respectively were on the viaduct to the right. BR Standard 'Clan' Pacific No.72004 CLAN MACDONALD with a 14–coach 'Starlight Special' from Gourock had just left the Paisley Joint at Shields Junction and was heading towards Terminus Junction and the Kilmarnock line. Meanwhile, after shunting Kinning Park goods, a Standard 3MT 2–6–0 waited to join the General Terminus branch which came in from the right. The 'Starlights' ran from 1953 to 1962 providing cheap overnight travel to London and until about 1960 were extremely popular in July and August when advance booking was essential. Most started from St. Enoch but there was a train from Gourock for several years and on this particular day one even originated at Clydebank Riverside and left Glasgow by the Lanarkshire & Ayrshire route through Kirkhill, Muirend and Neilston High.

Initially there were no intermediate stations between Bridge Street and Paisley, but in 1843 the Glasgow & Paisley Joint decided to provide platforms at Moss Road and Bellahouston. In marked contrast to the success of the line as a whole, these were a complete flop and closed in 1845. As the suburbs spread there was a second attempt and this proved justified. Ibrox station opened on the site of Bellahouston on 1st March 1871 and Moss Road was revived as Cardonald on 1st October 1879. Ibrox also served the Govan branch and eventually became a gateway for football fans heading towards the nearby Glasgow Rangers ground. Under gathering cloud, newly–outshopped Standard 2–6–0 No.76001 rested after bringing supporters from Springburn for an evening match on 22nd August 1962 as a decidedly grubby Standard 2–6–4T No.80109 added to the gloom as it thundered through with the 7.5 pm Glasgow Central – Gourock. The condition of the respective ex–LNER and ex–LMS rolling stock matched the engines. Ibrox station closed on 6th February 1967 and was swept away with electrification, but there is still a station on the Underground to cope with the football crowds.

A considerable amount of traffic on the Glasgow & Paisley Joint came from steamers serving coastal towns and villages along the Firth of Clyde. The Caledonian enjoyed a monopoly at Greenock until 1869 when G & SW trains began to run to Albert Harbour over the new Greenock & Ayrshire line through Kilmacolm. For two years there was a furious battle for traffic, but an agreement to pool receipts calmed the situation. However, in 1889 the Caledonian opened the line to Gourock and regained its supremacy. The G & SW fought back with faster boats and a sumptuous new station at Princes Pier, thus setting the scene for an exciting and colourful daily race for Glasgow customers which also involved the North British at Craigendoran on the north bank. World War 1 ended this extravagance and operations were afterwards more subdued. Following nationalisation Princes Pier lost its coastal steamers altogether but continued to deal with the transatlantic traffic which had begun in the 1920s. On 30th July 1955 ex–LMS compound 4–4–0 No.41142 piloted Fairburn 2–6–4T No.42229 through Ibrox with the 'Empress Voyager' boat train from Glasgow St. Enoch to Greenock Princes Pier in connection with Canadian Pacific's sailing that evening. The coaches carried roof boards, as did those for the 'Cunarder' departures. Although the train is using the slow line its only intermediate stop was Paisley Gilmour Street. The last boat train to Princes Pier ran on 30th November 1965.

Grimy Britannia Pacific 70052 FIRTH OF TAY left a trail of smoke across Pollokshields as it stormed through the Canal line platforms at Shields Road (the original Shields station) with a 'Starlight Special' from St. Enoch on 13th July 1962. This was Glasgow Fair Friday and other 'Starlights' from St. Enoch that evening ran via Barrhead and the Paisley Joint line. However, the popularity of the trains had waned, from a peak of a dozen or more, and they were not repeated in subsequent years.

LMS-built Fowler 2P 4-4-0s developed from an earlier Midland Railway design were drafted on to the former Glasgow & South Western system in considerable numbers during the late 1920s. They were very popular with crews and some of them were still working out their last days in 1961. Grimy, but with its full lining out still showing through, No.40643 left Berryknowes Road bridge behind as it barked out of Cardonald with the 6.0 pm from Glasgow St. Enoch to Dalry on 19th May 1960.

Traffic on the Glasgow & Paisley Joint line grew relentlessly as new branches were opened to the west and south – Kilmarnock (1843), Girvan (1860), Bridge of Weir (1864), Wemyss Bay (1865), Greenock Albert Harbour (1869), Stranraer (1877), Fairlie (1880). With the prospect of even further growth, the G & SW and Caledonian decided to add two more tracks to this section resulting in the only long stretch of quadruple main line in Scotland. Work was done in stages from 1880 to 1883 and involved the opening out of Arkleston tunnel and the reconstruction of Paisley Gilmour Street station. On 12th March 1966 BR Standard 2–6–4T 80045 waited for the road at Hillington East with the 15.15 Gourock to Glasgow Central as sister loco 80001 stormed through on the down fast line with the 15.57 Glasgow Central to Gourock. The route reverted to two tracks with electrification in 1967.

A six–car diesel multiple unit forming the 15.15 from Glasgow Central to Wemyss Bay on 12th March 1966 rushed past Hillington West on the through lines. This station was opened as Hillington on 1st April 1940 mainly to serve the adjoining industrial estate with its important Rolls Royce aero engine factory, but the residents of Penilee on the right also benefitted. The suffix West was added in March 1952. Hillington East, about half a mile nearer Glasgow Central, opened as Hillington on 10th March 1934 to serve the new Cardonald housing scheme in the distance. It gained its suffix when the 1940 Hillington opened. Both stations were very basic but they remain open and have a half–hourly service for most of the day with extra trains during the morning and evening peaks.

When the branch from Ibrox opened in 1868, shipbuilding was already established in Govan and streets of tenements were spreading inland from the river. During 1887 'bus trains' from Springburn, Bellgrove and Gallowgate began to venture along the line and the G & SW was confident about its superiority in the local transport scene. But 15 years later the situation had changed entirely and the company sent shock waves through the railway industry when it withdrew its half–hourly inner suburban service on 1st October 1902. This just could not compete with the cheaper and more frequent electric trams and the Subway which had provided a station nearby. Govan's large two–platform terminus finally closed to regular passenger services on 9th May 1921, but excursions still ran and the goods yard thrived for many years. Afternoon sunshine lit up the remains of the moribund station, the bulky Plaza cinema and a forest of cranes in the Harland & Wolff shipyard on 7th May 1955. Rail traffic finally ceased on 18th April 1966 and the site is now occupied by new car sheds for the revitalised Glasgow Underground.

Harland & Wolff's shipyard was served by a siding which crossed Govan Road near the Plaza cinema and was worked by an English Electric battery locomotive of 1936 vintage. Traffic to the neighbouring Fairfield Shipbuilding & Engineering Company yard was a much more complex and fascinating operation. A siding left the west side of Govan goods yard, then Fairfield's steeple cab electric used the tracks and overhead of tram routes 4, 7 and 27 along Govan Road for nearly 700 yards. With a Glasgow Corporation Leyland PD2 and a vintage Rolls Royce for company, the well-maintained loco turned into the yard with three wagons on 19th March 1958. Tram services 4, 7 and 27 were withdrawn on 6th September, 14th June and 16th March 1958 respectively – route 7 being replaced by trolleybuses. Revised overhead wiring served both Corporation and Fairfield needs until 1966. The steeple cab is preserved at Bo'ness and the shipyard now builds bulk carriers under the Norwegian ownership of Kvaerner Govan Ltd. Only two other yards currently remain on the Clyde – Yarrow at Scotstoun making frigates and Ferguson at Port Glasgow building ferries.

Another use of the tramways for railway purposes could be found ¾ mile west in Shieldhall. For a few hundred yards along Renfrew Road and Govan Road the tracks used by routes 4, 12 and 27 proved a convenient way of transferring wagons from Shieldhall Goods Depot to Alexander Stephen's Linthouse Shipyard. The Vale of Clyde Tramways Act of 1871 stipulated that provision had to be made for the passage of railway vehicles over the tram tracks, so a gauge of 4 ft 7¾in. was adopted – ¾in. narrower than standard railway practice. This allowed locos and wagons to travel on their flanges in the shallow 1¼in. groove where the tramcar wheels ran. In bright morning sunshine on 26th February 1958 Alexander Stephen's 1924 Andrew Barclay 0–4–0ST made its way towards the goods depot past 'Cunarder' tram No.1391 heading back to the city from Shieldhall on route 27. As noted at Govan, this ceased on 15th March 1958, followed by services 4 and 12 on 6th September and 15th November respectively. The tracks were retained for shipyard workings until the Linthouse complex closed in 1968.

Prince's Dock, originally known as Cessnock Dock, was built from 1886 to 1897 and stood immediately east of Govan. In an unprecedented spirit of co-operation, the Prince's Dock Joint line was a mutual venture by the Caledonian, Glasgow & South Western and North British, opening for goods traffic only on 17th August 1903. It curved away from the Govan branch at Ibrox, passed behind Glasgow Rangers' stadium and ran alongside Brand Street before turning into the docks under Govan Road. From here a Clyde Port Authority line made its way past Mavisbank Quay to General Terminus. Deep inside Prince's Dock, McIntosh 0–6–0 dock tank No.56159 from Polmadie shed shunted one of the many quayside sidings on 12th March 1956. Traffic had declined considerably ten years later and the joint line from Ibrox finally closed in 1970 followed by the docks themselves. The reclaimed site was used with flair for the Glasgow Garden Festival in 1988.

The first station on the Canal line west of Shields Road was Bellahouston & Dumbreck. At platform level it had large uninspiring wooden buildings only slightly enlivened by the canopy roof extensions carried on decorative iron brackets. Originally there was a pleasant chalet–like booking office (similar to that at Shields) on the Gower Street overbridge, but because of fire damage it was replaced by the worst sort of ugly brick block. In its heyday Bellahouston was the terminus for certain inner suburban trains, such as those from Bridgeton Cross in 1893–7, and there was a third platform face for this purpose. The station had been in decline for some time however when Dumfries 'Crab' 2–6–0 No.42913 hurried through with the 8.15 pm College to Dumfries goods on 3rd June 1954 and it closed 3½ months later, on 20th September. Bellahouston carriage sidings, glimpsed through the bridge, extended behind the platform to the left and survived in a much reduced form until the late 1980s.

Corkerhill was just a farm on the edge of Pollok Grounds when the G & SW decided to build new engine sheds alongside the Canal line. A staff halt consisting of timber platforms and tiny wooden buildings opened on 1st December 1896 to serve the depot and its associated railway village. It was publicly advertised from 1923 and in 1954 BR rebuilt the station with longer platforms, improved lighting and new brick and concrete buildings. Mosspark West, which opened in 1934 for new council housing at South Cardonald, received similar treatment. With the distinctive chimneys of the railway village in the background, Fairburn 2–6–4T 42124 pulled into Corkerhill on 18th September 1954 with the 2.30 pm Glasgow St. Enoch to Largs. The engine was shedded a few hundred yards away at 67A along with about 85 others including 'Jubilee', Black 5 and Standard 4–6–0s, Compound and 2P 4–4–0s, LMS and Standard 2–6–4Ts and an assortment of both tender and tank 0–6–0s. Corkerhill passenger locos worked to Largs, Ayr, Stranraer, Greenock Princes Pier and Carlisle via Kilmarnock.

The distinctive houses of Corkerhill railway village, some with half–timbered gables, others with brick gables capped by ball finials, were sadly derelict and awaiting demolition on 10th June 1969.

A superb stone aqueduct where the tracks crossed White Cart Water near Paisley was the most obvious clue to its origin, but the Canal line also pursued a level course, snaking with the contours in typical inland waterway fashion. BR Standard tank No.80128 took the curve between Kinnell Avenue and White Cart Water as it accelerated away from Corkerhill with the 5.13 pm Glasgow St. Enoch to Paisley West on 11th September 1964. Although Greater Glasgow PTE was keen to replace Kilmacolm – Glasgow Central trains with express buses, the Canal line won a reprieve in 1978 and again in 1979. Despite a massive campaign culminating in the TUCC pronouncement that closure would cause considerable hardship to school students and hospital visitors, the passenger service ceased on 10th January 1983. Tanker trains continued to run to Hawkhead oil terminal and Corkerhill became an electric depot in September 1984. By this time there were already plans for reopening the line to Paisley Canal and eventually on 28th July 1990 an hourly service of class 156 Sprinters commenced. On 30th November 1992 an 'Improved Paisley Pattern' was introduced to the Canal line with a half–hourly service provided by refurbished class 101 Metro Cammell diesel sets made up of two power cars. Hawkhead Oil depot closed in August 1992.

Crookston station was the most tragic victim of the closure saga. Its main building was long and very elegant with stone walls, deep round–headed windows and a big low–pitched roof sprouting neat chimneys. The most delightful feature was a wooden screen on the platform side with carved brackets supporting the eaves and petal–like fanlights. On 2nd September 1955 the fabric had accumulated 70 years of soot as Fairburn 2–6–4 tank No.42212 steamed through in charge of the 2.00 pm Largs – Glasgow St. Enoch. In 1978 the stonework was cleaned and platform areas tidied up, resulting in an environmental award. In 1982 Crookston's immaculate gardens led to a best–kept station prize. By the time passenger trains began to call again in 1990 the listed but abandoned building had been severely damaged by a deliberate fire.

Strathbungo was a small village alongside the road to Kilmarnock until it was engulfed by the growing suburbs of Pollokshields and Govanhill. Shortly after the Barrhead line became a main route to the south there was sufficient development to justify a station and this was opened on 1st December 1877. A large timber booking office was provided on Nithsdale Road and this was supported on metal columns with classical capitals, possibly in deference to the fine 'Greek' Thomson terrace overlooking the station from Moray Place. On 29th July 1955 ex–LMS 2P 4–4–0 No.40566 and Black 5 4–6–0 No.45118 had a full head of steam as they passed through Strathbungo ready to tackle Neilston bank with the heavy 7.55 pm 'Starlight Special' from St. Enoch. The pilot engine from Hurlford shed in Kilmarnock came off at New Cumnock. By 1894 the station was hemmed in by three others on the Cathcart Circle offering a very frequent service, but it stayed open until 28th May 1962. The street building survives as a shop and the cutting is still a verdant oasis.

With further suburban growth along Pollokshaws Road a station was provided at Crossmyloof from 1st June 1888 and it remains open today. In bright early evening sunshine on 24th May 1960 2P 4–4–0 No.40642 made a spirited start from there with the 5.43 pm Glasgow St. Enoch to Barrhead. At the time the goods yard looked deceptively busy, but it was mainly occupied by box vans used on the *Radio Times* traffic from Hairmyres near East Kilbride. Public facilities were withdrawn in November 1964 and after a small rail–served terrazzo plant closed in 1989 the yard became a car park for the new public house and refurbished tenements nearby. A year earlier the timber booking office and its supporting deck were removed and the original stone overbridge carrying Titwood Road was cleaned up. Ramps replaced the stairs and simple shelters succeeded the wooden platform buildings at the same time.

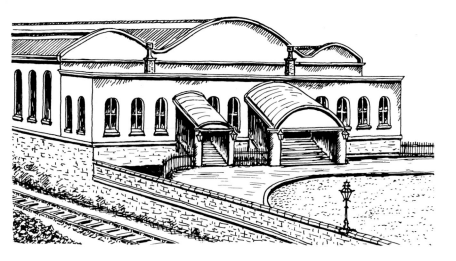

South Side station – once the gateway to England – with Gushetfaulds coal sidings in the foreground.

GLASGOW AND BARRHEAD

The second of the southern approach routes started off as a modest venture with an enigmatic title. On 29th September 1848 the Glasgow, Barrhead & Neilston Direct Railway opened its route from South Side station on the edge of Gorbals to Arthurlie Street in Barrhead. Eventually there was sufficient money to finish the project and 5th October 1855 saw the extension of the line to Crofthead which was renamed Neilston on 1st June 1868. In retrospect the 'Direct' part of the company name seems rather superfluous in view of the complete absence of competition at both Barrhead and Neilston until the early 1900s. Although superficially a purely local concern, the GB & ND was really part of the Caledonian's ambitions to reach Kilmarnock and therefore posed a threat to the Glasgow & South Western from the outset.

After nearly fifteen years of posturing by the two companies the G & SW broke ranks first and acquired powers for a line from Gorbals to Kilmarnock via Cathcart and Stewarton on 7th June 1865. This was associated with the City of Glasgow Union cross–city link and would have shortened journeys to Carlisle considerably. The Caledonian responded immediately by obtaining permission to extend the Neilston Direct to Kilmarnock. A fair amount of construction work ensued with the Caledonian building south from Neilston and the G & SW heading north from Kilmarnock. But in 1869 sanity prevailed and efforts were com-

bined in the form of the Glasgow, Barrhead & Kilmarnock Joint line which opened on 26th June 1873. Three years later a link from Langside Junction to the City Union at Gorbals Junction was completed. It smothered the original approach to South Side but enabled a London St. Pancras – Glasgow St. Enoch service to begin on 1st May 1876.

The Barrhead line was the most challenging route out of Glasgow on the south side. From low–lying Gorbals it reached almost 350ft. at Neilston and most of the climb took place beyond Pollokshaws, where 1 in 100 was the norm. Attractive stone bridges typical of railway practice in the 1840s were abundant, but perhaps the most endearing feature of the line was its succession of somewhat whimsical station names – notably Strathbungo, Crossmyloof and Nitshill. South Side station itself was little more than a wooden shed in the angle between Pollokshaws Road and Cathcart Road at first and as soon as it opened there were reservations about its suitability for local trains, let alone the English traffic which was about to descend on it from the Clydesdale Junction line. William Tite, famous for his classical termini at Nine Elms and Southampton, was commissioned to provide something better. The result was a compact but noble building presenting a fine facade to the Gorbals tenements. A train shed consisting of one main span flanked by two smaller ones ended in a screen wall which followed the curves of the roof line. In front of this was a lower office block with a flat roof, tall round headed windows and asymmetrical covered stairways. Most of the station was demolished to make way for the Langside Junction – Gorbals Junction viaduct, although temporary platforms for Barrhead and Motherwell local trains lasted until October 1877 and July 1879 respectively.

Pollokshaws was one of the original Glasgow, Barrhead & Neilston Direct stations, later gaining the appendage 'West' to distinguish it from facilities on the Cathcart Circle. Although mainly built of brick, a highly distinctive feature was the prominent decorative stonework for windows, doorways and corners. As the line ran on an embankment here, the main building facing Pollokshaws Road rose to two storeys externally. On the other side, in marked contrast to the built–up area, Pollok Grounds and White Cart Water provided an attractive wooded backcloth. Black Five 44992 called at Pollokshaws West in hazy spring sunshine with the 7.45 am Kilmarnock to Glasgow St. Enoch on 14th April 1966. Steam working ended shortly afterwards, but fortunately the station is largely unchanged.

Ex-LNER Thompson A2 Pacific 60522 STRAIGHT DEAL rolled across Boydstone Road bridge into Kennishead with the 11am from Carlisle to Glasgow St. Enoch on 9th January 1965. This was a somewhat humdrum duty for the former express engine as the train had called at almost every station and had taken some 3½ hours for the 115 mile journey. There had been a steady downpour most of the way and a blanket of cloud still hung over the distant Brownside Braes above Barrhead. To the left, Carnwadric Road follows the curve of the former Spiersbridge branch which opened with the main line and even had a passenger service until 1st May 1849. This proved a resounding failure, but in 1939 the LMS was ready to operate a Kennishead – Spiersbridge shuttle serving the new housing scheme at Arden until wartime austerity put paid to the idea. Goods traffic to Spiersbridge ceased in September 1941, but most of the branch remained in use until April 1964 to serve Thornliebank goods.

CLYDESDALE

As present-day expresses from London cover the last couple of miles into Glasgow Central they momentarily follow a railway route established nearly 200 years ago. William Dixon's tramway from Govanhill to the Ardrossan Canal basin at Port Eglinton was laid down in 1811 in order to help transport his coal and iron to Paisley. With wider markets in mind Dixon reconstructed his line and extended it eastwards to Rutherglen and northwards to the Clyde at Windmillcroft Quay. It reopened as the Polloc & Govan on 22nd August 1840 but remained isolated, horse–operated and increasingly out of step with railway developments elsewhere in Glasgow. This plodding existence continued until the Caledonian main line from Carlisle to Garriongill Junction was completed in 1848. At first trains approaching Glasgow had to use the roundabout route through Gartsherrie and Garnkirk and were received at the unsatisfactory Townhead terminus. The Clydesdale Junction Railway which opened on 1st June 1849 and incorporated part of the Polloc & Govan was an attempt to remedy this situation.

It left the Caledonian at Motherwell, spanned the Clyde beyond Uddingston and curved across undulating ground south of the river past Newton and Cambuslang. From Rutherglen the line followed the alignment of the Polloc & Govan through Polmadie before turning sharply north at Gushetfaulds to run alongside the Glasgow Barrhead & Neilston Direct to South Side station. Trains from Carlisle were immediately diverted on to the new branch, but the outer edge of Gorbals was hardly a convenient gateway to Glasgow for long–distance travellers and when Buchanan Street opened on 1st November 1849 the English expresses reverted to their original route. Over the next thirty years local passenger services from Motherwell, Hamilton and eventually Coatbridge ambled along the line and mineral traffic was important from the outset. The opening of Glasgow Central in 1879 elevated the Clydesdale Junction to main line status again and it has been the West Coast approach to the city ever since.

On 24th June 1861 a goods branch opened from Rutherglen to Dalmarnock on the far side of the Clyde. Although less than a mile long it was significant in having the first railway bridge over the river in the immediate vicinity of Glasgow. By April 1877 the rails had been extended another half mile to Parkhead and a Rutherglen – Dalmarnock – London Road passenger service began on 1st April 1879. Before long the branch became a convenient springing point for the Caledonian freight route round the north of the city and the Central Low Level underground line. A south–facing curve from Gushetfaulds to the Neilston line at Langside Junction opened on 29th January 1877, but the principal branch at the western end was finished in December 1848 and had to wait for the Clydesdale Junction to be completed. This was the General Terminus & Glasgow Harbour Railway which ran from the Polloc & Govan near West Street to the Clyde downstream from Windmillcroft. Lines had been projected from both the Garnkirk & Glasgow and Edinburgh & Glasgow down to the north bank but they failed to materialise and General Terminus gave the south side a monopoly of coal exports until the 1870s.

The enormous scale of the transformation of the modest Polloc & Govan into a main line approach is apparent in this view from Polmadie Road bridge. Polmadie motive power depot is on the left, Polmadie Yard fans out to the right and the North British Locomotive Company's Queens Park Works originally owned by Dübs was behind the camera. Polmadie loco shed opened in 1875 as a timber structure and was rebuilt in brick during the 1920s. It officially closed to steam on 1st May 1967 but serviced visiting engines from Carlisle Kingmoor for another eight months. Although the end of steam was still quite a way off, ex–LMS Jubilee 45613 KENYA was looking unkempt and had been given a fairly menial task in the form of the 9.10 am local from Carlisle to Glasgow Central, on 13th September 1963.

With Polmadie's yard lights already on, Pacifics 46245 CITY OF LONDON, 46231 DUCHESS OF ATHOLL and 46201 PRINCESS ELIZABETH were being prepared for overnight trains at about 8.30 pm, on 8th July 1959. Nocturnal duties for top link engines at the time were the 9.25 pm, 10.00 pm, 10.20 pm (sleeping cars only) and 10.25 pm to London Euston and the 11.15 pm to Birmingham New Street. A typical allocation at Polmadie in the 1950s was some 170 locomotives and the range was quite remarkable. There were Coronation, Britannia and Clan Pacifics for expresses and rebuilt Scots and class 5 4–6–0s for secondary main line work. Several dozen 2–6–4 and 0–4–4 tanks were maintained for Gourock, Wemyss Bay, Glasgow suburban and Lanarkshire locals. Goods engines varied from WD 2–10–0s and 2–8–0s to dock shunters and vintage Caley 'Jumbo' 0–6–0s.

As new docks opened lower down the river General Terminus was eclipsed to some extent, but with the increase in imported iron ore the quay was reconstructed to take bulk carriers and the first trainload was despatched on 7th January 1958. It was the beginning of a spectacular operation with double–headed WD 2–8–0s lifting 33 ton hoppers in rakes of 28 away from the river. Workings depended on the arrival of ships and often this involved departures in the early hours when the thunderous exhaust and violent slipping was especially noticeable and could be heard over a large part of Glasgow. Viewed from the Paisley Joint line platforms at Shields Road, WDs 90616 and 90199 got to grips with a train for Colville's steelworks at Cambuslang or Ravenscraig on 28th March 1959. In the background a bonded whisky warehouse on Seaward Street still had its own siding and loading platform but Scotland Street signal box, which controlled a connection to the City of Glasgow Union at Port Eglinton Junction, was boarded up and the line itself lifted. Iron ore workings ceased in December 1979 when Hunterston took over.

As usual, there was a lot of thick smoke drifting above Polmadie, in the warm summer evening air of 24th June 1960. Among the culprits being prepared for overnight workings on this occasion were Liverpool Bank Hall Jubilee DAUNTLESS, Camden Pacific CITY OF MANCHESTER and a very smart domestic Princess Coronation, No.46224 PRINCESS ALEXANDRA.

Although Polmadie never rivalled Edinburgh Haymarket for the immaculate condition of its Pacifics, a determined effort was made to turn out engines in a presentable condition – especially for prestigious trains such as the 'Royal Scot' – and a squad of retired drivers was recruited for this purpose. Outsiders were usually spruced up as well, and no doubt Coronation Pacific 46229 DUCHESS OF HAMILTON getting into its stride at Rutherglen with the 10.00 am 'Royal Scot' from Glasgow Central to London Euston on 24th September 1960 had received the treatment.

Rutherglen station dated from 1849 when the Clydesdale Junction line opened, but by 1895 it had acquired a triangular layout featuring nine platforms with no less than twelve faces, largely as a result of the impending completion of the Central Low Level system. On 11th March 1961 Fairburn 2–6–4T No.42244 paused at the through platforms on the original London Road branch with the 10.50am from Maryhill Central to the upland town of Strathaven.

Seen from Farmeloan Road bridge on 11th March 1961, Royal Scot 46107 ARGYLL & SUTHERLAND HIGHLANDER darkened an already leaden sky as it struggled past Dalmarnock Junction at Rutherglen with an exceptionally long rake of empty wagons. By then Polmadie's Scots had been displaced by English Electric Type 4 diesels on the Liverpool and Manchester trains, but this special working was proving more of a challenge than most expresses. With the West Coast electrification the station became an island platform and this was resited on the north to east curve during 1979 to serve Argyle line trains.

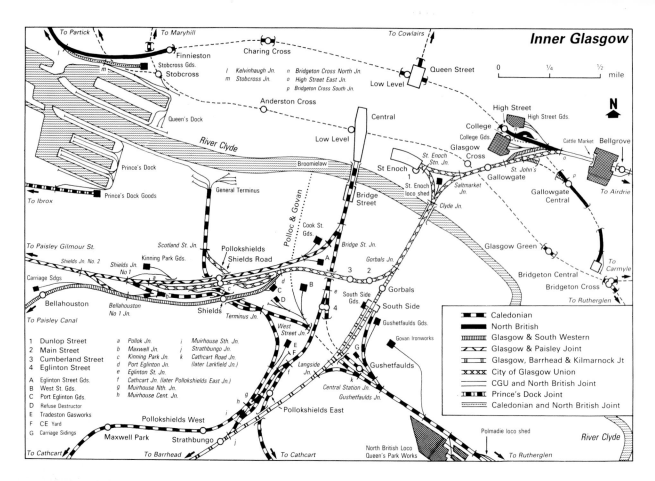

Inner Glasgow

1 Dunlop Street
2 Main Street
3 Cumberland Street
4 Eglinton Street

A Eglinton Street Gds.
B West St. Gds.
C Port Eglinton Gds.
D Refuse Destructor
E Tradeston Gasworks
F CE Yard
G Carriage Sidings

a Pollok Jn.
b Maxwell Jn.
c Kinning Park Jn.
d Port Eglinton Jn.
e Eglinton St. Jn.
f Cathcart Jn. (later Pollokshields East Jn.)
g Muirhouse Nth. Jn.
h Muirhouse Cent. Jn.

i Muirhouse Sth. Jn.
j Strathbungo Jn.
k Cathcart Road Jn.
   (later Larkfield Jn.)

l Kelvinhaugh Jn.
m Stobcross Jn.
n Bridgeton Cross North Jn.
o High Street East Jn.
p Bridgeton Cross South Jn.

Caledonian
North British
Glasgow & South Western
Glasgow & Paisley Joint
Glasgow, Barrhead & Kilmarnock Jt
City of Glasgow Union
CGU and North British Joint
Prince's Dock Joint
Caledonian and North British Joint

General Terminus had connections with each of the four main railways in the area. There was a link from the Glasgow & Paisley Joint between Shields Junction and Terminus Junction, although this involved a reversal. Far more important was the direct route from Gushetfaulds Junction on the Clydesdale line which brought traffic from the Lanarkshire coalfield. In 1870 when the first part of the City of Glasgow Union opened, the spur from Port Eglinton Junction to Scotland Street Junction was put in. The Glasgow, Barrhead & Kilmarnock had access over the branch from Muirhouse Junction to Terminus Junction and this passed close to Tradeston Gasworks. Barclay 0–4–0 saddle tank SCOTTISH GAS BOARD NO 1 built in 1920 was the gasworks pug and it had its work cut out lifting coal from the exchange sidings to the stockpile, as in this view looking south from Maxwell Road bridge on 25th May 1956. The tracks from Muirhouse Junction in the distance were used by passenger trains such as the Gourock 'Starlight Specials' and evening excursions from southern suburbs to the Clyde Coast via Terminus Junction and Shields Junction.

CITY OF GLASGOW UNION

Queen Street, Buchanan Street, Bridge Street and South Side were overstretched, inadequate or both by the 1860s and there was desperate need for a large central terminus in Glasgow. Furthermore a freight link across the Clyde between the Glasgow & South Western and Edinburgh & Glasgow systems was becoming a priority. These two companies had become friendly as a result of their mutual opposition to the Caledonian and consequently they promoted the City of Glasgow Union Railway, authorised on 29th July 1864 despite predictable and deep–rooted opposition from the Bridge and River Trustees. It was to consist of a 4¼ mile main line from West Street Junction on the Glasgow & Paisley Joint to Springburn on the Edinburgh & Glasgow's Sighthill branch with several spurs, including one to a grand passenger terminus facing St. Enoch Square. Before long the North British became the South Western's partner, having absorbed the E & G in 1865.

Not only was the City Union a difficult project physically, but it encountered enormous problems with land purchase and took twelve years to become reality. There were several amending Acts, notably the one which added ¾ mile to the western end by moving the Joint line connection to Pollok Junction beyond Shields Road. South of the Clyde the CGU ran on arches through Hutchesontown and Gorbals before the all–important river bridge just west of Glasgow Green. Beyond here a lot of valuable property had to be acquired for the viaduct across Bridgegate, Saltmarket, Glasgow Cross and Gallowgate, and land purchase for St. Enoch station itself proved exasperating. Shortly after Gallowgate the CGU joined the contemporary North British Coatbridge – College branch for a while before striking off on its own again towards Springburn. Most of the expense on the northern section was incurred by a succession of cuttings, tunnels and overbridges.

While the tedious wrangling for land at St. Enoch was going on, a temporary though substantial terminus was established at nearby Dunlop Street and from 12th December 1870 principal G & SW trains were diverted into it via Pollok Junction. On 1st June 1871 the 'bus trains' between Shields Road, Gallowgate and Bellgrove on the Coatbridge – College line commenced. The CGU began to carry through coaches between Edinburgh Waverley and various Ayrshire destinations on 1st September 1872 and three years later the northern section to Springburn opened for goods traffic. Possibly the most significant date for the City Union was 1st May 1876 when trains began to use the incomplete but already impressive terminus at St. Enoch. These included expresses from London St. Pancras via the Settle & Carlisle line and when the hotel was finished in 1879 Glasgow finally gained a magnificent station in the heart of the city, offering both domestic and English services.

On 29th June 1883 St. Enoch and its approach lines from Clyde and Saltmarket Junctions were transferred from City Union to G & SW ownership and the latter established its headquarters at the station. For ten years the CGU remained much the same, but then a rapid succession of developments established a pattern which lasted until the 1960s. The G &

SW finally withdrew from Bridge Street on 1st February 1892 but began running to the North British terminus at Bridgeton Cross in the east end on 1st April 1893. Access from the CGU was via a tunnelling spur east of Gallowgate station. Having served its purpose, the City Union was wound up on 7th August 1896 and its track apportioned to the G & SW and North British with the division at Sydney Street Junction (later High Street East Junction) on the Coatbridge line.

For a while the G & SW maintained its passenger service to Springburn in the northern suburbs and the North British (and indeed its successor the LNER) continued to run goods trains south of the Clyde to General Terminus and eventually Princes Dock. In 1898 the advertised service to Bridgeton Cross was abandoned, although workmen's trains

continued until 1913. Also in 1898, a substantial enlargement of St. Enoch and quadrupling from the station to Port Eglinton Junction where the Paisley Canal line and General Terminus connection came in gained parliamentary approval. The last Edinburgh – Ayr through working via the CGU ran on 30th September 1899 and 1st October 1902 saw the end of 'bus trains' from Govan, Paisley and Renfrew to Springburn. By this time the Bellgrove – Springburn line was an integral part of the North British suburban network and St. Enoch was the focal point of the G & SW system. The middle section of the CGU through Gallowgate had no regular passenger services but it remained important for freight and was frequently used by football and holiday specials.

Newton was an agricultural hamlet when the Clydesdale Junction opened, but it became a focus of heavy industry as well as a significant railway junction. Its station, dating from 1849, was rebuilt in 1973 and again in 1904 but after half a century of neglect the fine Caledonian platform buildings had become squalid, as was apparent in the long evening shadows of 9th July 1958.

The Rutherglen – Coatbridge line opened for passengers on 8th January 1866. Mount Vernon was the first of the four intermediate stations to close, on 16th August 1943, but the attractive timber buildings still stood on 11th May 1955 as Black 5 No.45162 ambled through with a westbound freight. Local passenger services ceased on 5th October 1964 but were due to be reinstated together with Mount Vernon station on 4th October 1993.

Shields Road and Gallowgate were the only intermediate stops along the City Union at first, but on 1st January 1872 trains began to call at Main Street Gorbals station which had been built on the viaduct near South Side. As a prelude to quadrupling it was replaced by Eglinton Street station immediately to the west on 1st October 1900 and these new facilities were designed on a lavish scale to compete with the nearby Caledonian premises of the same name. Heavy side walls supporting the overall roof rose almost as high as the adjoining four storey tenements and the main entrance block in Cumberland Street had Art Nouveau and Renaissance details in red sandstone. To avoid confusion the LMS renamed the station Cumberland Street in June 1924 at a time when it was the favourite gateway to the Clyde Coast for South Side residents. On 8th September 1955 McIntosh 0–4–4T No 55225 called with the 5.36 pm Renfrew Fulbar Street – Glasgow St. Enoch as the 6.5 pm St. Enoch – Largs passed through. By then the opulence was rather faded and most of the roof had been removed, leaving sturdy iron columns as supports for nothing more than telegraph wires and a waiting room with absurdly grand chimneys. The little piles on the platform were the result of enthusiastic weeding rather than burrowing creatures! Few trains called towards the end and access was by an apologetic entrance next to a pub in Eglinton Street. The doors finally closed on 14th February 1966 and most of the station was demolished when the line reverted to two tracks during the 1970s.

The City Union acquired powers for a line between Gorbals, Cathcart, Stewarton and Kilmarnock in 1865 but it was never built. Instead the Glasgow, Barrhead & Kilmarnock Joint was formed and a short connection from Gorbals Junction on the CGU to the GB & K just beyond South Side opened on 1st May 1876. Gorbals station next to the junction appeared in the timetable from 1st September 1877 as the replacement for South Side. It only survived until 1st June 1928, but the cut–back platforms were still there on 1st September 1964 as Black 5 No.45012 in charge of the 5.30 pm from Glasgow St. Enoch to Carlisle temporarily deprived Gorbals of sunshine. The four track section was a favourite racing ground for simultaneous departures from St. Enoch and on this occasion it was more or less a dead heat with the 5.30 pm diesel railcar to Ayr seen veering away towards Cumberland Street.

On 13th August 1965 Black 5 4–6–0 No.44707 in charge of the 17.33 from St. Enoch to Kilmarnock via Dalry easily outpaced Standard 2–6–4T No.80120 on the 17.33 to East Kilbride as the trains diverged at Gorbals Junction. As was clear from the figures leaning out of their respective cab windows, footplate crews clearly relished these unofficial races out of St. Enoch. No doubt quite a few passengers enjoyed the excitement as well! Similar contests took place between St. Enoch and Central trains on the four track Paisley Joint line.

Gallowgate, London Road, Saltmarket, Trongate and High Street converge at Glasgow Cross which was the commercial heart of the city until late Victorian times. Yet nearby Gallowgate station on the City Union viaduct was one of the first to close in Glasgow. Gallowgate opened on 19th December 1870 to handle North British trains from Coatbridge while their College terminus on High Street was completed. Within six months the 'bus trains' had started and eventually the station had frequent services linking Govan, Paisley and Renfrew with the east end and Springburn. When these ceased on 1st October 1902 Gallowgate closed as well, for there were electric trams in the streets below and Central Low Level trains below them. Parcels facilities continued and there was still one van a day until the early 1960s. Through traffic remained important, including football specials such as that from Springburn to Ibrox hauled by J39 0–6–0 No.64946 on 13th October 1956. Warehouses in Molendinar Street and tenements off Bell Street overlooked the cramped platforms, one of which had given way to a third track by this time. There are now firm plans for the reinstatement of passenger services and a new Gallowgate station, probably to be called Glasgow Cross, is part of them.

St. Enoch was officially opened by the Prince and Princess of Wales on 17th October 1876. It was the first large public building in Glasgow to be lit by electricity and had six platforms in three bays, each of which had a central carriage siding. This was more than adequate for the 80 trains a day which used it at first, but twenty years later there were over 500 cervices between 5 am and midnight plus light engine movements, summer specials and the Edinburgh – Ayr through coach transfers. The situation improved considerably with the 1901 extension which added another six platforms and a second arched roof – although this was slightly less grand than the original (70ft. high and 143ft. wide compared with 83ft. and 204ft. respectively). By this time the station had over 200 employees and handled 15 million passengers a year. On 4th June 1960 ex–LMS 2P 4–4–0 No.40669 was about to squeal round the sharp curve to Clyde Junction with the 11.30 am to Ayr as sister loco 40645 waited to join its train, having watered at the tank near the end of platform 1.

St. Enoch's most prestigious trains were the expresses to London St. Pancras via Carlisle, Leeds and Leicester. In 1902 there were departures at 9.15 am, 10.45 am and 1.30 pm with dining cars, 2.30 pm and 5.30 pm with seating accommodation only, and 9.30 pm and 11 pm with sleeping cars. Inevitably this generous provision could not be sustained in LMS and BR days, but at least the principal daytime service became famous as the 'Thames–Clyde Express'. It was a popular way of travelling from Glasgow to the West Riding and East Midlands or vice–versa, and when St. Enoch closed this one–time arch–rival to the Caledonian and LNWR route expresses ran from Central for a while. With an infuriating lack of headboard to complete the picture, ex–LMS 2P 4–4–0 No.40602 and Jubilee 4–6–0 45702 COLOSSUS were ready to leave St. Enoch in autumn sunshine with the 9.20 am up 'Thames–Clyde Express' on 5th November 1960. The pilot engine had clearly been stored for a while as the metal ring from the chimney bag was still in place. Maybe the Jubilee was pushing as well as pulling and no doubt there were some Bonfire Day fireworks, considering the condition of both locos!

Because of its close ties with both the G & SW and North British, the charismatic Midland Railway had a strong influence on the design of the CGU terminus. Gothic was the fashion, as at London St. Pancras in 1868, but a particularly sombre form was chosen for St. Enoch and ironically the style soon lost favour. The six storey hotel forming the station frontage opened in 1879 and its wall of Tudor windows capped by a forest of chimneys reared above St. Enoch Square. Even the glazed iron entrance veranda managed to look gothic and it led to a booking hall dominated by dark woodwork. The air of seriousness continued on the concourse where a large clock dominated a heavy destination indicator, supported on two kiosks facing platforms 2 and 3. At their outer ends the train sheds were finished off with great fan screens edged with spiky wrought iron decoration. Out in the open a number of particularly funereal little structures covered the stairways and parcels hoists from Dunlop Street. Amid this solemn architecture, Royal Scot 4–6–0 No.46117 WELSH GUARDSMAN prepared to leave platform 1 with the 4 pm express to Leeds City on 21st March 1959. St. Enoch received very little attention after 1901 and became even more gloomy as layers of grime accumulated. For the connoisseur of steam and Victorian gothic however, it was the most atmospheric station in Glasgow.

Specials were always an important part of operations at St. Enoch. Seaside excursions proved consistently popular during the summer and a glossy G & SW handbook advised golfers that they had their own services to the courses at Ayr, Troon, Irvine and Turnberry. Half a century later some of the heaviest trains to leave the terminus were the 'Starlight Specials'. With a keen south westerly breeze whipping smoke from the chimney after a heavy shower, Haymarket A3 Pacific 60100 SPEARMINT was about to leave platform 2 with the 8 pm departure for London Marylebone via Edinburgh Waverley on 11th May 1956. A smart set of coaches in 'blood and custard' was provided, and one or two people said their farewells to the overnight travellers. The building behind the engine housed first the City Union then the G & SW administrative headquarters. SPEARMINT was the regular engine of Haymarket driver Norman McKillop (alias 'Toram Beg'), as recounted in his 1958 book *Enginemen Elite*.

After inner suburban services were surrendered to the trams, the G & SW concentrated on its regular residential traffic from 30 to 45 miles out of Glasgow. For example, there were fast trains from Greenock, Ardrossan and Fairlie connecting with Firth of Clyde steamers, and in 1921 the 5.10 pm from St. Enoch ran non–stop over the 41½ miles to Ayr in 50 minutes. Forty years later there were still plenty of customers and on 15th June 1962 Black 5s Nos.45251 and 44977 stood at platforms 1 and 2 with 5.21 pm and 5.28 pm respectively to Largs. St. Enoch did not have a lingering death. When it closed on 27th June 1966 there were still 250 trains and 23,000 passengers every weekday to be transferred to Glasgow Central. Parcels continued until 5th June 1967, but afterwards there was a humiliating few years as a car park. The hotel closed in 1974 because it failed to comply with fire regulations and the whole site was cleared in 1975. It is now occupied by the vast St. Enoch Centre which has been received with mixed feelings.

GLASGOW CENTRAL

The original intention was to make St. Enoch available to any company wishing to operate passenger services into the centre of Glasgow, but Caledonian attempts to negotiate access before construction work began received a chilly reception. Although this was a predictable response from the blossoming Glasgow & South Western/North British alliance, there was also pressure from south of the border where the Midland Railway intended to win Anglo-Scottish traffic from the London & North Western – the Caledonian's ally in England. A final attempt when St. Enoch was nearing completion resulting in an exorbitant demand for £½ million for the privilege of running trains over City Union tracks. If it wished to have an effective presence in the city, the only option left to the Caledonian was to build its own bridge across the Clyde and its own terminus in the heart of the business district. Eventually the resultant Glasgow Central became one of the finest stations in Great Britain – but only after spasmodic problems with the G & SW at Bridge Street subsided and the original facilities on Gordon Street had been expanded and rebuilt.

Back in the 1840s the Clydesdale Junction wanted a terminus on the site later earmarked for St. Enoch. The River and Bridge Trustees, with support from Glasgow's citizens, thwarted this idea thus relegating the Caledonian to South Side. Thirty years later when public opinion had softened, the route north of here was already occupied by the City Union, so Bridge Street had to be the springing point and naturally G & SW cooperation at the joint station was minimal. The outcome was a restricted approach consisting of just two Caledonian through lines leading to a new Clyde bridge, a span across Argyle Street, and the eight–platform terminus fronting Gordon Street. Links were built to the Clydesdale and Barrhead lines and Bridge Street was rebuilt at considerable expense but with little effect, as noted earlier. Glasgow Central and its associated lines opened on 1st August 1879. Although there was plenty of dark woodwork in the station, the overall effect was less heavy than St. Enoch and the roof girders stretched away in a series of light horizontal spans rather than rising to a mighty arch. The frontage – built as Caledonian offices but immediately transformed into the Central Hotel – was an unlikely but happy combination of gothic, Tudor and Flemish styles.

At first the station had 134 services daily, so like St. Enoch it functioned quite adequately. By 1889 there were over 350 trains a day and platform 9 was added to cope with the extra traffic. In 1899 the number of weekday workings exceeded 480 and Central was congested despite the low level platforms which had opened in 1896 and took local trains from the industrial towns south and east of Glasgow. A drastic expansion of the terminus was essential and from 1901 to 1906 it was transformed in one of the most costly engineering projects ever undertaken by the Caledonian. A massive new bridge was built across the Clyde and the station itself was extended westwards towards Hope Street and Oswald Street and southwards towards the river. Platform space was doubled, with 1 to 9 being lengthened and new

ones numbered 10 to 13 provided on the west side together with a 30ft. wide cab road. The roof area was also enlarged considerably, this time using graceful semi-elliptical girders. Meanwhile Argyle Street bridge had become a tunnel. Initially there were loud protests but two dozen top quality shops and free shelter from inclement weather soon made it a social venue. After rebuilding, Central High Level was dealing with around 530 trains a day plus up to 150 extras at holiday times and some 25 million passengers a year used it.

Although the basic structure of Central has remained unchanged since 1906, the decor and facilities are very different nowadays. The Edwardian station had a wealth of glazed white tiles and opulent dark cabinetwork in rooms and passageways, and this has all but disappeared. Below the concourse was an enormous gents' lavatory with marble floors, heated copper towel rails and three sumptuous bathrooms. Advertisements were thought to detract from what the Caley offered so the only posters were railway ones. Train running information was provided on special slates which also showed the state of the weather at various points on the system. Perhaps the most delightful service was that offered by the 'Shop Parcels' department aimed at lady shoppers from out of town. After visiting Glasgow stores there was no need for them to struggle through the streets or hire a cab – a porter would collect their purchases while the customer indulged in afternoon tea at the station!

Central experienced piecemeal modernisation over the years, but drastic changes during the 1980s transformed it into the modern station greeting travellers today. In 1983 a £1 million travel centre opened and the former enquiry office was converted into a bar and restaurant. At the same time most of the old concourse kiosks were removed and a new marble floor was laid. A Casey Jones burger bar appeared in 1984 and the largest electronic train indicator in Europe costing £1¼ million was unveiled in May 1985. The vast and venerable manual indicator occupying the upper floor of a free standing torpedo–shaped building pointing towards platforms 8 & 9 was subsequently converted into a licensed restaurant, whilst a series of shops selling ties, socks and more intimate items of clothing opened as the Caledonia Centre. After a period tucked away in a corner the famous shell – one of Glasgow's favourite meeting places – was moved back to its rightful place in the middle of the concourse, emphasising Central's role as a social venue as well as a station.

Connections from the Barrhead & Kilmarnock Joint and Clydesdale Junction lines were a crucial part of the extension to Glasgow Central. The former originated at Strathbungo whilst the latter came off the General Terminus branch at Central Station Junction and immediately curved north in a tunnel under Pollokshaws Road. They met at Eglinton Street where a station consisting of four platforms on the main line and two more for the Kilmarnock route was eventually provided. Although this was in competition with the Glasgow & South Western's monumental edifice a few hundred yards away it consisted of a rather fussy collection of buildings and walkways on different levels. Looking south from Kilbirnie Street bridge on 9th May 1964, the 7.55 am 5–car diesel multiple unit from Carstairs to Glasgow Central was seen nearing the end of its journey with city shop and office workers. Cathcart Circle and East Kilbride trains used the elevated platforms to the right and the tracks curving between Maxwell Place and Milan Street in the background.

Although the City Union bridge across the Clyde was clearly a triumph over the river Trustees, it materialised as a sympathetic structure consisting of arched girders on masonry piers with more than a hint of the gothic shortly to emerge at St. Enoch. A new bridge was erected on the same site for the widened lines, opening in summer 1901. This displayed all the confidence of the age and a Derby 3–car diesel multiple unit forming the 09.05 from Kilmarnock to Glasgow St. Enoch on 28th August 1965 was dwarfed by the castellated sentinels at the north end as it turned towards the terminus at Clyde Junction. St. Enoch locomotive shed stood in the triangle between Clyde Junction, Saltmarket Junction and the station. Dating from 1884, it replaced Cook Street depot but declined in importance with the opening of Corkerhill; it was closed by the LMS in 1935. The substantial red sandstone building was then occupied by stored engines for a while and remained until the terminus finished, being used for engineer's materials at the end.

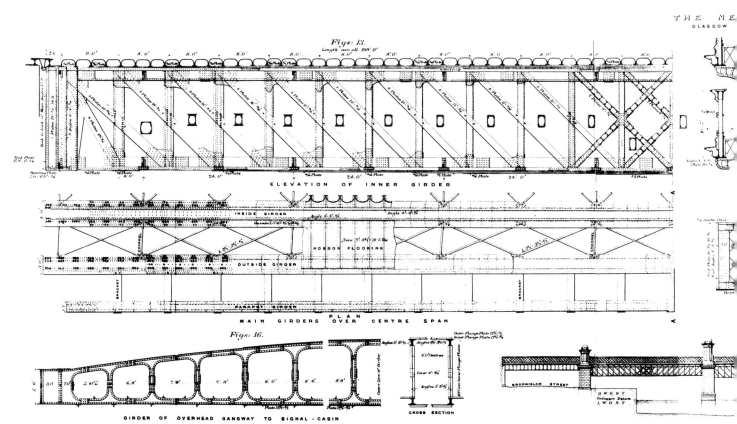

RIDGES

The original Clyde bridge leading to Glasgow Central was 700ft. long and carried four tracks. It consisted of five wrought iron lattice girder spans, three across the river itself flanked by others over Clyde Place and Broomielaw Street. These rested on cast iron cylinders sunk deep into the river bed which were faced with granite and linked by decorative iron arches to please the Clyde Trustees. The later bridge alongside it was 110ft. wide and carried 7 through tracks, although there were also several sidings and numerous crossovers. This time the steel girders were below the deck. Navigation clearance had to be maintained, so the rail level was 3ft. higher and the earlier bridge was raised accordingly. Viewed from the end of platform 9, un-rebuilt Patriot 4–6–0 No.45517 departed over the original bridge with the 4.10 pm relief to Manchester on 27th March 1959. In January 1961 resignalling and track rationalisation during the south side suburban electrification programme rendered the decaying 1879 spans redundant. A move that would have astounded the old Clyde Trustees came in 1987 when the surviving viaduct was painted burgundy, blue, charcoal, gold and white and floodlit at night!

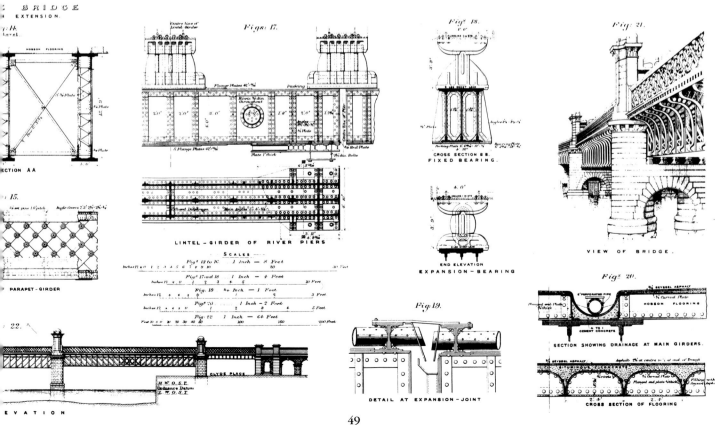

Eglinton Street station was provided with long and spacious platforms in anticipation of brisk suburban business, but road transport ensured that it never got anywhere near its full potential. In the brief moment when Polmadie Pacific No.46231 DUCHESS OF ATHOLL rolled under Kilbirnie Street bridge with the London Euston – Glasgow Central 'Royal Scot' on 19th May 1955 there were no less than three trams and one bus in Eglinton Street itself to the left. The station closed on 1st February 1965 just before its equally moribund ex–G & SW neighbour and virtually all traces of it were subsequently removed. Even the buses have few customers in Eglinton Street nowadays, for the tenements have been demolished as well.

Some named expresses had a very short lifespan and one of these was 'The Caledonian'. The inaugural train departed from Glasgow Central at 8.30 am on 17th June 1957 hauled by 'Coronation' Pacific No.46229 DUCHESS OF HAMILTON, a Camden engine at the time. The down working left Euston at 4.15 pm and was due to pull into Central at 10.55 pm. Platform 3 was used and had a suitably inscribed archway. Although the driver and fireman of McIntosh 0–4–4T No.55207 on station pilot duty at platform 9 were full of admiration, 'The Caledonian' was withdrawn after its schedule had been lengthened as a result of electrification work between Euston and Crewe in the early 1960s.

The unique BR Standard class 8P Pacific No.71000 DUKE OF GLOUCESTER from Crewe North shed was in charge of the 1.30 pm 'Mid–Day Scot' at platform 2 on 23rd September 1954. Although the engine was only a few months old, this particular Glasgow to Euston connection dated back to Caledonian and London & North Western days when it was known as 'The Corridor'. The name 'Mid–Day Scot' was introduced by the LMS in 1927 and was perpetuated by British Railways, but it had fallen out of use by 1970. Platform 2 was (and still is) the main departure point for expresses from Central. In the background the fine iron tracery and aisle–like double row of columns separating the 1879 and 1906 roofs provide an aptly elegant setting.

Ever since Glasgow Central was enlarged, it has not been uncommon for two or even three departures and a similar number of arrivals to take place at about the same time. Close (though not quite simultaneous) departures could be seen together on 15th August 1959. Standard 4MT 2–6–0 No.76071 eased out of platform 8 with the 12.11 pm to East Kilbride as Fairburn 2–6–4 tank No 42695 prepared to leave platform 9 with the 12.14 pm to Uplawmoor. Over towards Jamaica Street four young lads were hoping for an invitation on to the footplate of Jubilee 4–6–0 No 45668 MADDEN as it waited at platform 1 with the 12.25 pm to Lockerbie. On the right another Fairburn 2–6–4 tank stood in the short refuge provided for locos awaiting their next passenger turn. Between duties most engines went to the carriage sidings at Bridge Street just across the Clyde, Larkfield beyond Eglinton Street or Smithy Lye near Shields Road, whilst others returned to Polmadie.

Even with assistance from its low level platforms the terminus has always had to cope with a large number of local services. In Caledonian days the Clydesdale Junction line alone was used by trains to Coatbridge, Airdrie, Hamilton, Strathaven, Stonehouse, Lesmahagow, Coalburn, Bothwell, Motherwell, Holytown, Wishaw, Shotts, Newmains and Lanark. Most departures from Central were fairly cautious because of the numerous points and signals, but ex–Caledonian 'Jumbo' 0–6–0 No.57419 made a particularly determined start from the east side with the 8.20 pm to Strathaven on 9th June 1954. Beyond platform 1 there was an engine refuge known as the Colosseum Siding and the origin of the name was the department store advertising itself prominently behind the smoke. The building represented by the round—headed window above the tender was making a far less brazen show of itself, but this is the iron–framed Gardner's warehouse of 1856 which proved a landmark in European architecture.

Ex-Caledonian Pickersgill 3P 4–4–0 No.54477 was in charge of the 7.53 am from Lanark to Glasgow Central on 26th March 1957 and the train is seen here on arrival at platform 4. Prominent are the hydraulic buffers designed to stop a 400 ton train at 12 mph in 7 feet without shock. The spaciousness of Central is apparent from this viewpoint and the difference between the original and extension roof styles can be seen as well. Virtually all of the station stood some way above ground level and was built over an undercroft, the decking consisting of rolled steel girders resting on brick piers and covered with 8 inches of concrete and ¾ inch of asphalt. Ease of crowd movement was paramount in the 1901–6 rebuilding and there were staggered platform ends as well as curved walls and rounded corners for the concourse buildings, as is evident in those still remaining.

Some 'Central' stations were not always as conveniently located as their name suggested, but the suffix was entirely justified in the case of Glasgow for there was access from four of the city's main thoroughfares. The northern frontage on Gordon Street had the hotel and the main entrance featuring an ornate glazed canopy over the cab pull–in. Hope Street to the west had the carriage driveway as well as two doorways and there were two more in Argyle Street under the bridge. Union Street to the east had a big, flamboyant 'Art Nouveau' entrance – seen to the right of Coronation tram No.1217 on 1st June 1960 as it worked route 3 from Mosspark to Park Road via Charing Cross three days before the service was withdrawn. Above the car is the Egyptian Building with its heavy cornice and remarkable colonnade of bulbous stubby pillars. On the left 'Carswell – The Modern Man's Shop' no doubt had to adapt its window display as the 'Swinging Sixties' progressed!

This aerial photograph taken on 25th September 1991 shows both the evolution of Glasgow Central station over the previous 112 years and the changes wrought on the city centre generally over the last three decades. The 1879 station can be identified by the glazed roof towards the bottom right of the view with ridges parallel to the tracks, whilst the pairs of columns rising from the Clyde to the bottom left are a reminder of the original approach bridge abandoned in 1961. The huge 1901–6 expansion involving new platforms on the west side, an extension of the earlier canopy and a second bridge over the river, are clearly seen from above. Also notable is the significant curve where the 1879 alignment was slewed on to the newer bridge in 1961. Argyle Street strikes top left to mid right under the broadest part of the station and the Central Low Level tracks run beneath it. Part of the glass envelope which replaced St. Enoch station is in the bottom right hand corner and the tiny isolated building just outside it is the erstwhile entrance to the Underground, which runs parallel to the Central main line tracks at this point, but far below them. About half of the Victorian buildings in this slice of the city centre have already been replaced by modern structures, but tower cranes indicate that the process continues – although the original facades tend to be kept nowadays. Broomielaw Quay, used for many years by steamers to and from the Clyde coast, is to the right of Central station bridge.

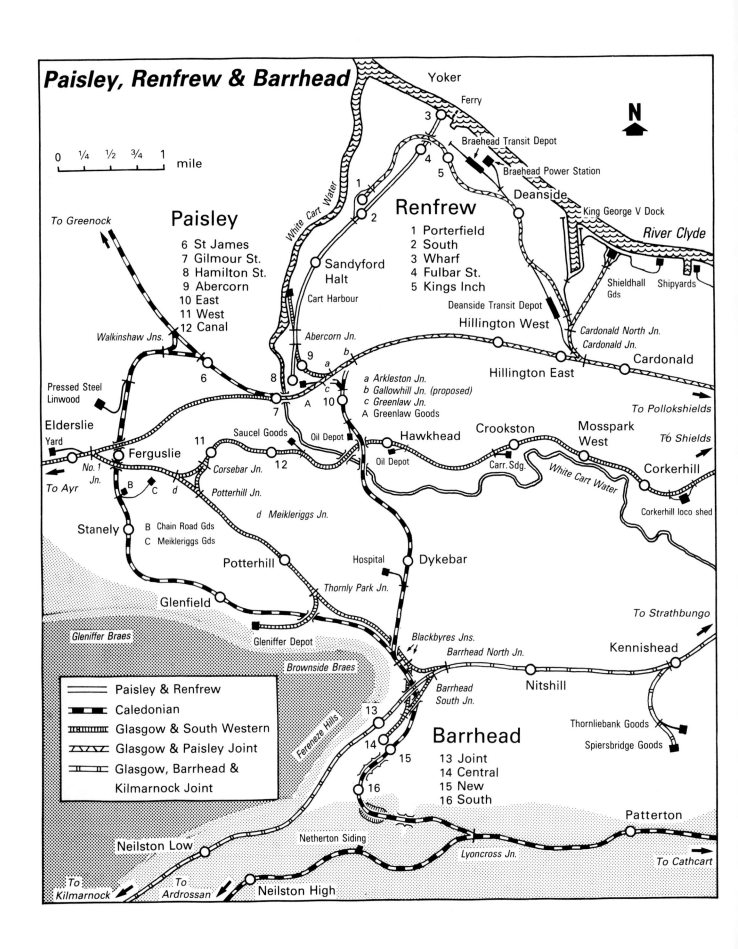

Paisley, Renfrew & Barrhead

N

0   ¼   ½   ¾   1   mile

To Greenock

Paisley

6 St James
7 Gilmour St.
8 Hamilton St.
9 Abercorn
10 East
11 West
12 Canal

Yoker

Ferry

White Cart Water

Sandyford Halt

Cart Harbour

Walkinshaw Jns.

Renfrew

1 Porterfield
2 South
3 Wharf
4 Fulbar St.
5 Kings Inch

Braehead Transit Depot
Braehead Power Station
Deanside
King George V Dock
River Clyde
Shieldhall Gds
Shipyards

Deanside Transit Depot
Hillington West
Cardonald North Jn.
Cardonald Jn.
Cardonald

Abercorn Jn.

a Arkleston Jn.
b Gallowhill Jn. (proposed)
c Greenlaw Jn.
A Greenlaw Goods

Hillington East

To Pollokshields

Pressed Steel Linwood

Elderslie
Yard

Ferguslie

No. 1 Jn.

To Ayr

Saucel Goods

Oil Depot
Oil Depot

Hawkhead

Crookston

Carr. Sdg.

Mosspark West

To Shields

Corkerhill

White Cart Water

Corkerhill loco shed

Corsebar Jn.

Potterhill Jn.

d Meikleriggs Jn.

Stanely

B Chain Road Gds
C Meikleriggs Gds

Potterhill

Glenfield

Gleniffer Braes

Gleniffer Depot

Brownside Braes

Fereneze Hills

Hospital

Thornly Park Jn.

Dykebar

To Strathbungo

Kennishead

Blackbyres Jns.
Barrhead North Jn.

Nitshill

Barrhead South Jn.

Thornliebank Goods
Spiersbridge Goods

Barrhead

13 Joint
14 Central
15 New
16 South

Patterton

To Cathcart

Netherton Siding

Lyoncross Jn.

Neilston Low

Neilston High

To Kilmarnock

To Ardrossan

Legend

————— Paisley & Renfrew
▬▬▬▬ Caledonian
▭▭▭▭ Glasgow & South Western
▰▰▰▰ Glasgow & Paisley Joint
═╪═╪═ Glasgow, Barrhead & Kilmarnock Joint

Paisley, Renfrew and Barrhead

Some seven miles west of Glasgow Central three towns stand in an arc between the River Clyde and the uplands of Mearns. Renfrew occupies gently rising ground east of the mouth of White Cart Water. Although it has been dominated by shipbuilding and engineering in recent times, this Royal Burgh and erstwhile county town of Renfrewshire had a civic status on a par with that of Dumbarton and Glasgow in medieval times. Paisley sits astride White Cart Water at its tidal limit about 3 miles inland from Renfrew. Over the years the town has been famous for shawls, thread, marmalade and poets and is dominated by surviving parts of a great Cluniac Abbey – the nave (now constituting the parish church) and the Place of Paisley. Two miles south the sandstone of the Clyde valley gives way to hard volcanic rocks forming the Braes which rise rapidly to over 700 feet. In the lee of these, on a tributary of the White Cart called Levern Water, stands Barrhead. It once depended on engineering and calico printing, but later became known for Shank's potteries and sanitary equipment works, the products of which could be seen in numerous stations.

Although Paisley, Renfrew and Barrhead are just about joined to the suburbs of Glasgow nowadays, they remain distinctive communities in their own right and regard themselves as separate from the city. But from the railway point of view the three towns have always been part of the Glasgow network and form a natural boundary of the system in the south west. First came the Paisley & Renfrew which was

almost as old as the Garnkirk & Glasgow and was also built for purely local needs. The three links with Glasgow came next, and the Paisley Joint, Barrhead & Neilston Direct, and Canal line proved the most durable routes in the area. Finally, at the turn of the century, there was a remarkable and largely misguided upsurge in construction. The district gained a plethora of new suburban lines which proved hopelessly over–optimistic for passenger traffic and only survived because of goods.

PAISLEY & RENFREW

Despite the fact that White Cart Water was navigable as far as Paisley, the proprietors of the Paisley & Renfrew Railway envisaged a healthy trade in both passengers and merchandise. Their single track route was built across almost featureless country from a terminus in Hamilton Street (in Paisley) to Renfrew Wharf on the Clyde. It opened on 3rd April 1837 to the 'Scotch' gauge of 4ft. 6in. and was quite impressive for its day. Three Glasgow–built 2–2–2 locomotives were employed and Hamilton Street station in Paisley possessed a sizeable timber train shed. However, when the Glasgow & Paisley Joint opened in 1840 the Renfrew line suffered an eclipse and decided to abandon its steam engines and resort to horse traction during 1842. On 24th July 1847 it was taken over by the Glasgow, Paisley, Kilmarnock & Ayr and thus became Glasgow & South Western property in 1852. Under its new owners the Paisley & Renfrew remained horse–worked, self–contained and largely irrelevant

for several years. But increasing industrialisation of the area eventually demanded something better.

On 1st February 1866 the line was completely closed so that it could be converted to standard gauge double track. Hamilton Street passenger terminus was abandoned, an eastward–facing spur to the Glasgow & Paisley Joint line was installed, and handsome new stations were built at Paisley and Renfrew. Steam returned on 1st August 1866 when a through service from Renfrew to Glasgow Bridge Street was inaugurated. The trains were transferred to St. Enoch ten years later. In 1874 the main line connection was moved further east to Arkleston Junction, giving a more sweeping curve, and the old formation was eventually covered by Greenlaw goods yard. Gradually the open space between Renfrew and Paisley was taken up by industry with the result that two new stations appeared; South Renfrew opened on 1st May 1897 and Sandyford Halt appeared in June 1914, as a private platform for Ogston and Tennant's factory. Workmen made up a sizeable proportion of Paisley & Renfrew passengers and became even more important after the trams took away most local traffic. Towards the end trains ran almost exclusively for workers and the meagre timetable reflected this. After an unassuming but very long life, the passenger service was withdrawn on 5th June 1967. Steam traction was still in use until the end of April, a diesel multiple unit taking over the workings for the last six weeks.

A bank of cloud was building up over the distant Kilpatrick Hills as a couple of rakes of ex–LMS suburban coaches stood in the early morning sunshine at Renfrew Wharf on 7th December 1955. Even then the island platform had a woebegone look about it; most branch trains started from nearby Renfrew Fulbar Street station anyway, but passenger traffic had another 11½ years to run. In this view from Meadowside Street bridge, Yoker Power Station dominated the far bank of the Clyde. Off to the right was the chain ferry, sometimes described as a large floating greenhouse, whilst straight ahead behind the coal bank was Yoker Ferry station, on the Lanarkshire & Dumbartonshire line. A tug was moored at the site of the actual wharf which was still used by steamers from Broomielaw until it was virtually destroyed in a World War 2 air raid. Buchanan's oil depot at Renfrew Wharf was rail served until the end of 1977 but by 1980 all traces of the terminus had been obliterated. Across the river, the power station has also been flattened.

The station which replaced Hamilton Street terminus in Paisley eventually gained the suffix Abercorn. Its two storey main block and smaller wings were constructed of sandstone and had very low–pitched roofs sprouting a forest of distinctive chimneys. Originally there was also a projecting canopy. The contemporary building at Renfrew Fulbar Street had similar features, although it was single storey throughout. In 1936 the line from Paisley to South Renfrew was singled and one side of Abercorn station was taken out of use. On 31st July 1958 2P 4–4–0 No.40636 pulled into the remaining platform at Paisley Abercorn with the 5.36 pm Renfrew Fulbar Street – Glasgow St. Enoch. After a stifling day in factories and foundries everybody was eager to get home and most compartment doors were swinging open in anticipation of the rush to Gilmour Street station or the bus for the suburbs. Goods traffic continued over most of the line after 1967 and official closure from Arkleston Junction to the Babcock & Wilcox works just beyond Sandyford Halt did not come until 5th January 1981, although there had been no traffic for some time.

Most boats continued to sail up White Cart Water to Paisley rather than dock at Renfrew Wharf and this contributed to the parlous state of the Paisley & Renfrew Railway in its early years. Facilities for coastal shipping at Paisley were improved substantially when Cart Harbour opened in 1891 and a branch from the Renfrew line was taken down to the quayside. Rail access ceased in March 1965 and the tracks were overgrown when STORMLIGHT, one of the last Clyde Puffers, set sail on 17th September 1966. Cart Harbour closed in 1967 and is now silted up. There have been proposals to relay the branch and construct a bridge over White Cart Water to give access to Glasgow Airport.

THE GLASGOW LINES

Three of the lines approaching Glasgow from the south passed through the Paisley – Barrhead area and they provided stations at Paisley Gilmour Street, Barrhead, and Paisley Canal respectively. The first of these stood at the junction of the Glasgow, Paisley, Kilmarnock & Ayr, which was completed along the Black Cart Water valley on 21st July 1840, and the Glasgow, Paisley & Greenock, which provided a link with the Clyde Coast from 31st March 1841. A service along the Glasgow & Paisley Joint line to Bridge Street had begun on 14th July 1840. Barrhead station was where the Glasgow, Barrhead & Neilston Direct terminated short of its destination in the Mearns from 27th September 1848. On 5th October 1855 the GB & N was extended to Crofthead which was renamed Neilston in June 1868. That station closed on 1st May 1870 but there was a replacement from 27th March 1871 when the Glasgow, Barrhead & Kilmarnock Joint reached Stewarton just north of Kilmarnock. Finally, having twisted its way along the contours from Shields Road, the G & SW replacement for the Ardrossan Canal reached Paisley Canal station, which opened on 1st July 1885.

Paisley Gilmour Street, originally a modest two platform affair with a Tudor–style entrance at street level and indifferent timber waiting rooms, was rebuilt in 1883 on a generous scale. On 3rd October 1955, Pickersgill 4–4–0 No.54468 struggled away from the ex–G&SW side of the station with the 12.17pm Greenock Princes Pier – Glasgow St. Enoch in a cloud of escaping steam.

Although the Glasgow, Barrhead & Neilston Direct was a modest concern, it provided a particularly good station just over a quarter of a mile from the centre of Barrhead. With its low–pitched roof and large overhangs the main building facing Carlibar Road was vaguely reminiscent of contemporary practice over the border, in certain parts of northern England. It was finished in smooth sandstone with very prominent chiselled quoins or corner stones. Stubby chimneys in groups of two or three stood out yet still maintained the low profile of the structure, and canopies carried on projecting brackets or supported by iron columns displayed some attractive wood carving. Viewed from the bridge over Arthurlie Street on 14th July 1962, BR/Sulzer Type 4 diesel D24 pulled into Barrhead with the 5.3 pm Glasgow St. Enoch to Kilmarnock. This was a filling–in turn for the loco between express duties along Nithsdale and over the Settle & Carlisle.

Canal station was just under half a mile uphill from The Cross which marks the centre of Paisley. Steeply sloping ground and a certain amount of constriction resulting from its waterway ancestry combined to create an awkward site. The main building was off to the left on Stow Place and a timber structure with carved brackets, generous glazing and flamboyant fanlights, more than making up for its diminutive stature, faced Causeyside Street. On 27th April 1957 Standard tram No.258 climbed past the station on its way from Renfrew Ferry to Glenfield. There were plenty of people walking and a notable lack of private cars on this bright spring day, but route 28 was doomed, the last trams running a fortnight later.

In marked contrast to its main road frontage, the bulk of Paisley Canal station was dominated by stonework. Although the hefty side walls and broad slabbed platforms were rather bleak, some exquisite details and an overall elegance made the long range of buildings on the north side one of the finest G & SW compositions. It was a dismal evening on Friday 30th August 1963 as BR Standard 2–6–4 tank No.80021 ambled in with the 6.48 pm from Kilmacolm to Glasgow St. Enoch. In this view from the steps up to Causeyside Street the little group on the platform includes a couple of pensioners with a suitcase, no doubt setting off on holiday. The station closed with the Canal line passenger service on 10th January 1983 and adjoining goods facilities, by then just a coal yard, finished on 23rd January 1984. When trains to Glasgow Central began again on 28th July 1990 they used a single platform on the opposite side of Causeyside Street. Meanwhile the main building had been refurbished as a restaurant.

SUBURBAN MANIA

The spate of suburban railway construction around Paisley began modestly with a short branch which climbed from the Canal line west of the town to a hamlet called Potterhill, on the lower slopes of the Brownside Braes. It opened for goods traffic on 5th February 1886 and a passenger service from Paisley Canal commenced on 1st June. During 1899 an even more steeply graded extension took the line in a sweeping curve up to Glenfield yard adjacent to Fulton's textile mills, where coal was delivered and finished products taken away. By then the stage was set for The Mania and rival schemes to link Paisley with Barrhead were already under way.

Glasgow & South Western engineers had the easier task and their route opened first. From Thornly Park Junction, mid–way along the Glenfield extension, double track rounded the eastern flank of the Brownside Braes, passed under the Kilmarnock line half a mile short of Barrhead joint station, bridged the Levern Water and terminated at a new station, Barrhead Central, on the north side of Mill Road. A spur was put in so that trains from the joint line had access to Barrhead Central and there was also an avoiding line from Blackbyres Junction to Barrhead North Junction. On 1st October 1902 the G & SW began to run a Glasgow St. Enoch – Barrhead Central passenger service which went out via the Kilmarnock route and returned along the Canal line, or vice versa. This brave venture managed to survive just five years of debilitating competition from the parallel tramways.

The Caledonian attempt to provide Paisley and Barrhead with a circular service was considerably more ambitious and proved to be even more of a disaster. It began with the nominally independent Paisley & Barrhead District Railway which was authorised in 1897 and absorbed by the Caledonian during 1902. The new line left the Greenock route at Paisley St. James station about a mile beyond Gilmour Street and soon turned south to pass under the G & SW Ayr and Canal tracks in quick succession. It continued to climb through Stanely and Glenfield just below the steep face of the Braes and encountered its rival near Thornly Park. The G & SW and Caledonian jostled for position all the way to the centre of Barrhead where the latter built an imposing high level station called Barrhead New (the town had thus acquired three stations more or less side by side) on the opposite side of Mill Road to Barrhead Central. From here the line headed for West Arthurlie, passed through a precipitous rock cutting near Springhill Road, crossed a ravine on a viaduct and joined the newly–built Lanarkshire & Ayrshire Railway at Lyoncross Junction, between Patterton and Neiston High. The 1897 Act also sanctioned a branch from the Glasgow & Paisley Joint line east of Gilmour Street station to the route from Paisley St. James at a second Blackbyres Junction alongside the G & SW. After crossing White Cart Water just outside Paisley this line faced a fierce two mile ascent round the slopes of Dykebar Hill to reach Blackbyres.

So Paisley and Barrhead acquired a comprehensive suburban network with seven stations, thanks largely to the Caledonian. Besides the local circular service involving a reversal at Barrhead New, it was intended that trains would run from Glasgow Central to Barrhead via the Lanarkshire & Ayrshire to Lyoncross Junction, continue to Gilmour Street, and return along the Glasgow & Paisley Joint – or vice versa. That was the theory. In fact as the system neared completion the Caledonian decided that it was the electric tram rather than the G & SW which was its true competitor here. Goods traffic began in June 1905 but Board of Trade approval for passenger services was never sought. Furthermore, the line from Barrhead South to Lyoncross Junction stood unused until it was lifted in 1917 and connections with the Glasgow & Paisley Joint were never made, leaving Paisley East goods yard at the end of a ludicrous 8½ mile branch from the other side of town. As described later the stations remained in their unopened state for many years.

While the Barrhead saga was unfolding to the south, Renfrew also acquired another passenger service and this proved slightly more successful – but only just. The Glasgow & Renfrew District Railway was built by the Glasgow & Paisley Joint to stimulate industrial development in remote flatlands bordering the Clyde between Govan and Renfrew. It ran from Cardonald North Junction on the existing Shields branch to a terminus at Renfrew Porterfield, adjacent to South Renfrew station on the Wharf line. An hourly passenger service began on 1st June 1903 calling at Deanside and Renfrew Central, which became King's Inch after a month. Trains were worked by the Caledonian and G & SW for alternate six month sessions, but the former pulled out in 1907. The LMS saw little point in competing with itself for the fairly sparse passenger traffic at Renfrew and withdrawal took effect from 19th July 1926. Fortunately there was sufficient demand from industry in Renfrew to keep the line in business.

Just west of Paisley the Canal line abandoned the course of the former waterway and headed off towards Elderslie on the Ayr route. This was also the site of Corsebar Junction where the branch to Barrhead Central began. On 1st June 1897 Paisley West station opened at the same point, and having terminated there with the 5.46 pm from Glasgow St. Enoch on 27th April 1957 ex–Caledonian 'Standard Goods' 0–6–0 No.57241 ran round its train on the Barrhead tracks. In the distance the Gleniffer Braes rise to 779ft. at Thornliemuir and beyond the cricket match an embankment leads the G & SW suburban branch towards its 1 in 70 climb through whinstone cuttings on the face of the Braes. Paisley West closed on 14th February 1966, passenger trains from Kilmacolm finished in 1983, and the line from Hawkhead oil depot through Paisley to Elderslie closed officially on 10th November 1984.

Potterhill station, seen here in use as a house on 10th August 1955, opened on 1st June 1886 and was virtually identical to Crookston on the Canal line. Unfortunately such architectural excellence was hardly justified in this case. The circular service from Glasgow St. Enoch which began on 1st October 1902 was abandoned on 1st October 1907 and the track was singled in 1909. Potterhill retained through trains to St. Enoch via Paisley and even had a shuttle to Barrhead Central until 1st June 1913, but the wartime withdrawal of passenger facilities on 1st January 1917 proved permanent and trains from Glasgow terminated at Paisley West from then on. Goods traffic to Gleniffer Depot – which Glenfield had been renamed in 1923 – continued until 4th May 1959 and a Cadbury–Fry warehouse on Neilston Road near Potterhill station was rail–served until the mid–1960s.

Barrhead Central was an attractive and well–appointed small terminus by any standards. Its main building adopted the Jacobean revival style which had been in vogue for some years, and it was a particularly fine example. Authentic narrow bricks were complemented by abundant stone dressings including a plinth above the pavement, a string course above the windows and capping for the parapets. Delightful Dutch gables overlooked the approach, one with an intricate medallion, the other broken by a chimney and featuring a circular window. There were little finials at each corner, a big semi–circular porch hood and superb Tudor windows. The station faced a square known as The Centre and on the right Mill Road dropped away towards Levern Water. Also off to the right an island platform occupied an increasingly lofty embankment and it was covered throughout its length and width by a glazed canopy featuring deep valances and supported on pairs of iron columns. There were run–round loops either side of the platform tracks. This view was a commercial postcard stamped 9th July 1904. At the time the optimistic circular service to Glasgow St. Enoch ran, but complete closure after the period of retrenchment came on 1st January 1917. Barrhead's delightful G & SW station was finally demolished in 1950. Photograph Barrhead and Neilston Historical Association.

Evidence of mis-spent Caledonian money was everywhere on the Paisley & Barrhead District. The line was fully signalled yet its boxes were never manned and at first a signalman travelled on the goods trains to operate levers as required. All seven stations were built as well. Apart from the bloated affair at Barrhead New and bleak Barrhead South where only the side platforms were made, they consisted of a generous island platform with a modest building and were provided at Ferguslie, Stanely, Glenfield, Dykebar and Paisley East. Ferguslie actually managed a few passenger trains in the form of Sunday School specials to the Clyde Coast before it was demolished about 1950. Paisley East station on Glasgow Road made way for the large Kelbourne cinema in 1928. The other three were let as dwellings. Drummond Standard Goods 0–6–0 No.57288 posed alongside the overgrown platform at Stanely on 12th March 1960. By this time suburban Paisley had engulfed Stanely and Glenfield stations and the trams had gone, but it was far too late for the railway to compete with the replacement bus services.

There was still frost on the sleepers and a cold fog hung over Boghead and the featureless Black Cart Water meadows as McIntosh 0–6–0 No.57622 approached Ferguslie with the daily freight from Greenlaw Yard to Barrhead South on 22nd March 1960. The ten box vans were probably destined for Paisley East, the four open wagons served local coal merchants and the eight tankers were dropped at Hawkhead siding. The train had just rounded the curve from Walkinshaw West Junction.

Approaching Barrhead the suburban rivalry between the Caledonian and G & SW was emphasised by parallel running. With a cheerful grin from the fireman, ex-Caledonian McIntosh '812' 0–6–0 No.57555 loped towards Blackbyres Junction with the early afternoon freight for Barrhead South on Boxing Day 1958. Harelaw Crossing in the foreground is about 200 feet higher than Paisley and a brisk wind from the Braes snatched smoke from the engine. The former G & SW route to Barrhead (closed completely when the passenger shuttle from Potterhill finished in 1913) was down in the shallow cutting immediately to the right. Although a short train of five mineral wagons was understandable for December 26th, the gasworks at Barrhead South and oil depot at Hawkhead normally provided a large amount of traffic, which sometimes required double heading.

With the granite setts glistening from steady rain, Standard tram No.293 negotiated the sharp corner and steep downhill slope from Main Street to Arthurlie Street in the centre of Barrhead. It was 29th September 1956 and although the trams were in their twilight years they had at least served the town for over half a century, unlike the ill–fated Caledonian suburban route across the lattice girder bridge. The Paisley & Barrhead District line climbed steeply away to the left towards Barrhead South on a long curved masonry viaduct. Off to the right, 200 yards away in Mill Road, Barrhead New station on the Caledonian line once squared up to the G & SW Barrhead Central terminus. Within a couple of minutes the tram would have passed Barrhead's other station which had served the town for over a century and continues to do so, albeit rebuilt rather frugally. Apart from a length of viaduct off to the left alongside Kelburn Street, all traces of the Caledonian route have been erased from the town centre, but the inn continues to offer hospitality.

Although much demolition had taken place, the sheer scale of Barrhead New station is still apparent in this extremely rare photograph taken about 1930. The projecting central section of the 1904 frontage was originally twice as high as this and rose to gable ends which reared above Mill Road. Fashionable details were employed, such as glazed bricks for the lower parts of the walls and little Baroque mouldings under the flat arches above the doorways. 'Caledonian' was announced confidently in metal letters on horizontal bars and 'Barrhead New' could just be discerned above the booking office windows. Apart from a touch of stonework around the doorways, concrete seems to have been chosen for the bulk of the structure. Adjoining wings had towering ribbed walls more akin to a medieval fortress than a station. An interesting glimpse of social history is the daubed slogan 'Vote ILP' on the planking over the middle window and a poster for the local Independent Labour Party candidate. This grossly extravagant building was never used for any purpose, let alone railway passenger services. Photograph Caledonian Railway Association.

This is how Glasgow's initial batch of 'Blue Trains' made their first journeys. Ex–Caledonian McIntosh 'Standard Passenger' 0–4–4 tank No.55225 hauled one of the brand new electric sets from the Pressed Steel works at Linwood past Ferguslie Park on 6th June 1960. New diesel multiple units for the Western Region were being delivered at the same time, but they left under their own power. The associated Rootes car factory started production in 1961 and gave the northern part of the Paisley & Barrhead District line an extra lease of life. Amid controversy, the then owners Chrysler decided to close the plant in 1981, and the last Talbot Sunbeam rolled off the production line at the end of May. The branch remained in situ for 3½ years, but redevelopment of the Linwood site for retail warehouses and a garden centre makes its reinstatement unlikely.

Although passenger traffic ceased in 1926, a certain amount of commercial development did eventually take place alongside the Glasgow & Renfrew District line. Braehead and Deanside Transit Depots were built during World War 2 for the distribution of goods brought in by sea, and Braehead Power Station opened in 1951. On 19th March 1958 ex–Midland 4F 0–6–0 No.43996 passed Deanside propelling four wagons of steel tubes from Cardonald North Junction to Braehead. Deanside station, like King's Inch and Porterfield, had a large island platform but it was a total failure and closed to passengers on 2nd January 1905 and freight in October 1926. In 1964 the line was closed from Porterfield to Braehead and cut back further to Deanside Transit Depot in 1977.

Probably the most important enterprise served by the Glasgow & Renfrew District was King George V Dock, which opened in July 1931, just down river from Shieldhall goods depot. Further deep water docks were planned along the mile of undeveloped riverside to Renfrew but economic uncertainties followed by World War 2 ensured that they never materialised. One outcome of the war was that King George V Dock gained a passenger platform which was used by troop trains. On 13th March 1956 ex–Caledonian McIntosh 0–6–0 tank No.56361 shunted the quayside overlooked by a couple of Clan Line freighters. Although some tracks remain, traffic to the Clyde Port Authority facilities around Shieldhall is now very sparse.

Blue Funnel Line cargo vessel JASON left King George V Dock bound for the high seas on 8th September 1954 attended by tugs FORAGER, WARRIOR and CRUISER. The first ship to use the dock when it opened on 10th July 1931 was a Blue Funnel steamer. This famous concern was registered in 1865 as the Ocean Steam Ship Company by Alfred Holt who rightly predicted that the combination of a compound engine, screw propeller and iron hull would be ideal for the Far East trade. By 1875 Blue Funnel was operating 14 ships to China via the Suez Canal and had added routes to Japan and Jeddah within another ten years. Although the company was still operating passenger liners to Asia in the early 1960s, its name faded away in the fog of takeovers and containerisation during the 1970s and 1980s.

South Side Suburban

When the Paisley, Barrhead and Clydesdale lines were opened, Glasgow had barely begun to spread south of the river. Some development had taken place at Pollokshields and Gorbals, but the tracks to Bridge Street only had four streets to cross before reaching the Clyde, and South Side station was on the edge of the built up area. Beyond lay open farming country with a scattering of villages, several of which had water–powered textile mills. At first the land sloped gradually towards low yet prominent hills at Pollok and Langside, but then suddenly rose to the Cathkin Braes over 600 feet above the city. On their western flank the White Cart Water had carved a profound cleft as it tumbled down from the high moors of Cunninghame through Busby and Cathcart.

In the 1840s this was infertile ground for railway passenger traffic. But today a huge slice of suburban Glasgow occupies the angle between the Barrhead and Clydesdale routes and it supports a network of local lines, with stations every half mile or so and frequent services. Development of the southern suburbs began in earnest at Govanhill, some two miles south of the city centre, during the 1870s and has continued ever since. The tenements of Pollokshields and Queen's Park came first, followed by the villas of Langside and Giffnock. Vast municipal estates at King's Park, Croftfoot and Castlemilk pushed the city boundary towards the Cathkin Braes and small private developments are still filling some of the gaps. Nevertheless, the relationship between suburban growth and suburban railways on the south side was not a particularly straightforward one. The earliest line was built to serve local industry but soon attracted residential properties, the second deliberately set out to stimulate suburbia, and the third was conceived as a mineral route, from coalfield to coast, soon becoming enmeshed in the corporation housing schemes.

THE BUSBY RAILWAY

In the mid–1800s Busby, some seven miles out to the south east, had a flourishing cloth printing works alongside the White Cart Water and was one of the more important Cathkin textile villages. Two miles away at Giffnock large quarries supplied sandstone for building Glasgow's tenements and commercial properties as well as slabs of limestone for paving its new streets. The Busby Railway was promoted locally, primarily to exploit these industries, and its 3½ mile branch from Pollokshaws on the Glasgow, Barrhead & Neilston Direct was authorised on 11th May 1863. It opened on 1st January 1866 with a four mile extension to the farming village of East Kilbride following on 1st September 1868. The main engineering work was a five arch viaduct over the White Cart Water in a deep ravine just before Busby. Otherwise the most significant feature of the line was a relentless climb up the Cathkin slopes, from approximately 100 feet above sea level at Pollokshaws to 300 feet at Busby and 500 feet at East Kilbride. Besides working goods and mineral traffic the Caledonian ran a modest passenger service of three trains a day to Busby and East Kilbride from South Side.

This proved sufficient to encourage a few people to forsake the city and build villas near the railway, a trend which grew rapidly. Demand soon began to outstrip line capacity and the original single track beyond Giffnock was doubled as far as Busby on 22nd December 1881. The Caledonian absorbed the local company on 1st February 1882 and in 1885 extended the branch to High Blantyre near Hamilton where it joined existing tracks. Over the next twenty years villages were virtually transformed into dormitory settlements and prior to World War 1 there was even a non–stop morning business train from Busby to Glasgow Central. Meanwhile the textile mills closed and Giffnock's worked–out quarries stood as gaping pits waiting to be filled with ironworks slag.

East Kilbride was designated a New Town in 1947 and promised to sustain traffic, but the branch was not included in the suburban electrification programme and there have been closure threats on several occasions. The most serious came in 1964 and might have succeeded had it not been for a spirited defence by the East Kilbride Railway Development Association. A scheme to divert trains via a spur to the Neilston line at Clarkston and close Giffnock and Thornliebank stations arose in 1983 but the opposition triumphed again. With the introduction of class 156 Sprinters in 1990 there was a sharp upturn in patronage and the future is considerably brighter.

Thornliebank was also well known for printing cotton when the Busby Railway opened, but in this case the village had to wait until 1st October 1881 for a station. By this time residential development was proceeding apace and eventually the built up area extended west to Carnwadric, north to Mansewood and east to Orchard Park. But there was still plenty of greenery about on 22nd August 1959 as Fairburn 2–6–4 tank No.42696 blasted up the severe gradient out of Thornliebank with the 12.11 pm Glasgow Central – East Kilbride. It was a sweltering day and nearly all the compartment windows were dropped on the five LMS non–corridor coaches. The route indicator over the buffer beam showed the code for the East Kilbride line. Argus Foundry beyond the road bridge opened about 1920 and had railway sidings until its closure in 1963. Somewhat unusually, Thornliebank's goods station was on the Spiersbridge branch, about half a mile away. Freight traffic continued to East Kilbride until January 1984.

On 28th May 1964 Standard 2–6–4T 80116 pulled into Giffnock with the 5.33 pm from Glasgow St. Enoch to East Kilbride. The steep climb from Pollokshaws continued here and the last blast of smoke before the driver eased off the regulator drifted away in an easterly breeze. The branch to Giffnock's extensive quarries went away to the right behind the elegant signal box of mid–Caledonian vintage. By this time the route codes had gone and Standard BR non–corridor stock had virtually replaced the LMS coaches.

Station buildings on the Busby Railway were neat single storey structures more typical of a Borders branch line than suburban Glasgow. An attractive combination of chiselled and smooth Giffnock stone was employed and the larger ones had heavy but highly decorative cast iron brackets supporting the canopies. The tiny building at Clarkston was particularly charming but it was superseded by a new station just to the south when the line was doubled in 1881. Nevertheless it survived together with a stretch of overgrown platform, albeit dwarfed by a four storey tenement which the proprietors of the Busby Railway could hardly have envisaged. In low early morning sunshine Standard 2–6–4 tank 80058 cast smoke shadows over the former station as it passed with the 8.18 am commuter service from East Kilbride to Glasgow St. Enoch, on 25th June 1964.

On 28th March 1966 the 17.08 from Glasgow St. Enoch to East Kilbride climbed away from Busby dutifully carrying city workers back home – including the photographer who uncharacteristically had no chance to record the number of the Standard 2–6–4 tank! St. Enoch station and Busby goods yard both closed three months later; steam traction only had a year left in Glasgow, but the East Kilbride branch itself had just been reprieved when the Minister of Transport refused his consent for closure on 7th January. At the time Busby had about 20 all–stations services to the city. However, in 1993 there were nearly 40 trains to Central as well as a morning express from East Kilbride which did not stop. Although the wooden building on the staggered 1881 down platform was destroyed by fire in 1965, Busby's original block still exists and retains its canopy and its character despite being converted into a Chinese takeaway. The station house and goods shed also survive.

Canopy detail at Maxwell Park.

CATHCART CIRCLE

It looks fairly insignificant on a map – just a 5½ mile loop serving the inner suburbs south of the Clyde. But the Cathcart Circle was more than just a suburban railway. It became part of Glasgow folklore and was even celebrated in a highly entertaining novel. The Circle leaves the Kilmarnock line at Pollokshields, climbs through Crosshill to reach Mount Florida and Cathcart, almost doubles back on itself to follow the White Cart Water, then heads back to Pollokshields and joins the Kilmarnock line almost where it began. In the process it encircles Queen's Park which celebrates the nearby Battle of Langside, where the army of Mary Queen of Scots was defeated. The Cathcart Circle had its own

battle with electric trams soon after completion, but despite several lean periods it has continued to serve the south side since the mid–1890s.

The Circle line started as the Cathcart District Railway, authorised in 1880, its 2¼ mile branch from the Caledonian's Bridge Street – Strathbungo line opening as far as Mount Florida on 1st March 1886 and through to the single platform terminus at Cathcart on 25th May. Most of it passed through open country but both the local company and its Caledonian backers had shrewdly anticipated the spread of suburbia towards the Cathkin Braes. Approval for the completion of the Circle came in 1887 and the extension through Langside and Maxwell Park together with a new station at Cathcart came into use on 2nd April 1894. In effect the double track carried separate Inner and Outer Circle services from Glasgow Central, giving passengers a choice of trains to and from the city. Within a few years houses surrounded each of the ten stations, fully justifying the capital outlay on the line. The Cathcart District remained nominally independent until 1923 although the Caledonian worked it from the outset.

Before World War 1 there was an intensive timetable of about 45 trains a day on each circle from 6.00 am to 11.30 pm, and from 1903–4 the eastern section had to cope with those on the new Lanarkshire & Ayrshire routes to Ardrossan and Newton as well. Hostilities meant a reduction in frequency and the Cathcart Circle never completely recovered. By the mid–1950s services were down to

roughly 30 weekday trains on each circle and from July 1958 the last departures from Glasgow Central were cut back to 7.30 pm. Matters improved with electrification on 29th May 1962 – this did not prove a panacea and there was another bout of evening economies during the 1980s. Although late trains have been reinstated there were only around 20 workings each way on the Circle during the early 1990s, reinforced by Newton and Neilston services.

R.W.Campbell's *Snooker Tam of the Cathcart Railway* published in 1919 presented a colourful picture of the Circle during World War 1: *"A wag has alleged that this railway was specially built 'for high heid yins in insurance offices, public hooses, and drapers' shops'. No matter! It is a most convenient line, and the cheapest thing out of Lipton's. For fourpence you can ride round and round the Circle. Indeed, many a lover has found that it is better to invest fourpence in the Cathcart Circle than two shillings at the picture–house. It is a deadly trap for bachelors, and the hope of pretty typists. All single men, on arriving in 'Glesca' are advised to look for lodgings round the Circle. No wonder! At 'the five––thirty' can be seen everything from a Geisha to a Madonna. The Venus from Pollokshields rubs shoulders with the Gaby from Cathcart."*

Snooker Tam is the station boy at imaginary Kirkbride where romance blossoms with ticket girl Maggie McCheery – despite the tiffs. Maister McMuckle, Puddin' Broon, Jimmy McCloon and Conkie McBeetle are encountered along the way as are wee servant lassies who look round the office door and ask, 'Ony persels for the hoose?' Life on the south side has changed as much as the Circle itself.

A wide variety of trains have served the Cathcart Circle over the years. Before the 1923 Grouping most of them consisted of rakes of 4-wheel carriages hauled by 0–4–4 tanks, but main line engines – including the mighty 'Cardeans' – were rostered on fill–in turns or for turning purposes. The LMS introduced new non–corridor bogie coaches and during the 1950s Fairburn and BR Standard 2–6–4 tanks gradually displaced ageing Caley locos. Prior to electrification diesel multiple units and the occasional Glasgow Central – Edinburgh Princes Street Inter–City set mingled with steam on the Circle. Following Grouping the ex–Glasgow & South Western shed at Corkerhill worked certain Cathcart trains and on at least one occasion sent a massive Whitelegg 4–6–4 tank. This tradition continued and on 24th April 1957 Corkerhill 2P 4–4–0 No.40570 was seen from Albert Drive bridge heading the 5.57 pm Glasgow Central to Whitecraigs. Pollokshields East Junction (originally Cathcart Junction) in the background where the Cathcart District left the Bridge Street – Strathbungo line remains much the same, albeit renamed yet again as Muirhouse North, but the antique cart on the bank no doubt passed into oblivion long ago.

Pollokshields East station was on the edge of one of Glasgow's most fashionable districts when the line was built, although Tradeston Gasworks in the background and Coplawhill Car Works on the right hardly gave that impression as veteran McIntosh 0–4–4 tank 55189 arrived with the 4.30 pm from Glasgow Central on 14th March 1956. The route indicator over the right buffer identified it as an Outer Circle train – Inner Circle workings had the V pointing the opposite way. All ten stations on the Cathcart District had island platforms and most of them featured a tall single storey building with a fine umbrella canopy supported by beautifully carved wooden brackets. But this particular one witnessed a tragic and sinister event one evening in December 1945 when the female clerk on duty was shot dead and the junior porter mortally wounded. There was fear and apprehension on the south side until October 1946 when a 20 year old railway fireman gave himself up to Glasgow police. He was sentenced to death, commuted to life imprisonment, but was killed in a car crash just after his release.

The ¼ mile section between Pollokshields East and Queen's Park was one of the most awkward parts of the Cathcart Circle to build. First came a 1 in 70 drop below the St. Enoch – Barrhead line, followed by a 1 in 70 rise through Strathbungo, where streets of tenements were already established and the railway picked a route through them in a deep walled cutting. Several roads had to be carried over the tracks by broad girder bridges. In this very atmospheric view of Queen's Park on 16th May 1956 the 4.30 pm Outer Circle service was hauled by an ex–Caledonian 0–4–4 tank again and a young lad admires No.55201 basking in the sunshine. Despite electrification the station has retained its character and the elegant tenements of fawn Giffnock stone in the background still peer down from Torrisdale Street.

Beyond Queen's Park the line ran along the southern fringe of Govanhill, then curved sharply south at Crosshill station and headed towards Mount Florida. Middle class housing developments quickly followed the arrival of the railway. During the evening peak, crowded Outer Circle trains began to empty noticeably by Mount Florida, although the rush had yet to start when Standard 2–6–4 tank No.80027 called with the 3.30 pm from Glasgow Central on 26th October 1955. However, there were three football grounds nearby and the influx for important marches overshadowed ordinary traffic. Even Queen's Park and Third Lanark had specials at one time but Internationals at the vast Hampden Park stadium required a carefully planned operation.

Snooker Tam of the Cathcart Railway (from
the cover of R.W. Campbell's book).

On 14th April 1956 Scotland played England at Hampden Park and there were no
less than twenty specials from Glasgow Central alone. After supporters had
alighted at Mount Florida, trains ran empty round the Circle and some returned to
the carriage sidings at Bridge Street. Others were stabled at Muirhouse in the
engineer's yard or the Tradeston Gasworks exchange sidings next to the Strathbungo – Shields Junction line. The latter were usually the preserve of the gasworks
'pug' but were cleared of wagons for such occasions. At the end of the match
normal services on the Inner Circle were suspended and the specials took over.
They were lined up buffer to buffer from Cathcart North Junction back along the
Inner Circle to Pollokshaws East, then hand signalled one by one into Mount
Florida. Prior to this, the view from Albert Drive revealed Standard 5MT 4–6–0
No.73058 ready to leave and 2–6–4 tanks Nos.80002, 42193 and 80112 in the sidings
building up steam ready for their respective departures. The whole business went
off without a hitch and railwaymen accepted it as part of the day's work.

The intense suburban passenger service on the Circle tended to overshadow other types of traffic, but as late as 1938 an Ardrossan boat
train called at Cathcart and a pick–up goods continued after electrification. Although physical constraints ruled out freight facilities at
most stations there were yards at Pollokshaws East, Mount Florida and Maxwell Park until 1959, 1961 and 1964 respectively. Cathcart's
sidings survived until April 1965 and after shunting the yard McIntosh 3F 0–6–0 tank No.56305 ambled through the station with the daily
Outer Circle goods on 28th October 1955. In marked contrast to the earlier stations, Cathcart is above street level and the northern end of
the platforms are actually on a bridge spanning White Cart Water. Tenements featured prominently in the expansion of Cathcart but
further west there was ample building land and two storey villas flank the track for over a mile. As a result Langside station has a
spacious air about it and this is helped by the fine view of Cathkin Braes. Pollokshaws East is equally elevated and looks down on the
White Cart Water again from an impressive stone arch.

The remaining stations were exceptionally interesting even by Cathcart Circle standards. Shawlands was decidedly peculiar, for part of the platform spanned Pollokshaws Road and Rossendale Road in quick succession and the intervening space beneath the tracks was occupied by two railway houses. The choice of rough–hewn stone and Baronial trappings reminiscent of a Highland castle was very appropriate in view of the regular hammering on the ceiling! But Maxwell Park and Pollokshields West displayed Caledonian architecture at its most beautiful. Both were built in a long cutting bordered by Fotheringay Road and Terregles Avenue with access by lattice footbridges from street level. Consequently the standard Cathcart District design was elevated to two storeys and formed an exquisite composition, especially when viewed end on. The slender wooden buildings had steep roofs supported on splayed brackets and capped by finial–like chimneys, with the familiar glass canopies forming an elegant apron. After an overnight blizzard Maxwell Park could have been mistaken for an Alpine halt on 25th February 1958, as Fairburn 2–6–4 tank No.42277 disturbed the crisp sunny morning with the 9.30 am Outer Circle train.

The ten Cathcart District station buildings have experienced mixed fortunes. Five have been demolished and the replacements vary from bus shelters at Langside to a new brick and timber structure emulating its predecessor at Mount Florida. Queen's Park and Crosshill are virtually unaltered and Cathcart retains its authentic appearance despite extensive rebuilding a few years ago. Maxwell Park and Pollokshields West are both listed buildings but since de–staffing in 1985 they have been alone and neglected. The former is still intact despite attempts to burn it down, whilst BR itself began to demolish the latter until ordered to stop. Ten days before the end of steam, Standard 2–6–4 tank No.80130 departed from Pollokshields West with the 12.30 pm Outer Circle train on 19th May 1962.

LANARKSHIRE & AYRSHIRE

The suburban branches to Neilston and Newton were electrified on 29th May 1962 at the same time as the Cathcart Circle and serve a number of large housing estates. But when the Neilston – Cathcart – Newton line was being built at the turn of the century it passed through open country below the breezy Cathkin Braes, and passenger traffic was a minor consideration. In fact the Lanarkshire & Ayrshire Railway came almost too late for its intended purpose and within 30 years had taken on a very different role in the Glasgow area. Because of inadequate loading facilities on the Clyde, a large amount of coal was being taken from Lanarkshire to the Ayrshire port of Ardrossan by the 1880s. However, the Caledonian was obliged to hand it over to the Glasgow & South Western at Gushetfaulds, barely a third of the way into the journey. The Lanarkshire & Ayrshire, which eventually gave the Caledonian a totally independent route to the docks, originated in 1888 as a modest line to Ardrossan from Barrmill on the Glasgow, Barrhead & Kilmarnock branch to Beith. Mineral traffic was diverted to the jointly owned Kilmarnock line, but the Caledonian still begrudged the G & SW its share of the takings. An extension of the L & A from Barrmill through Uplawmoor, Neilston and Cathcart to Newton on the Clydesdale Junction line was authorised on 23rd July 1897, by which time the Caledonian was firmly in control of the local company. The Barrmill – Cathcart section opened for goods on 1st April 1903 and passengers on 1st May, with access for Caledonian coal trains via Hamilton, East Kilbride, and a spur off the Busby Railway at Clarkston. Finally, a direct route from the Lanarkshire collieries was provided by the Cathcart – Newton line which carried freight and passengers from 6th January and 1st August 1904 respectively. A steady procession of coal trains stormed up the 1 in 100 from Cathcart to Neilston at first, but this proved a brief spell of glory for the L & A. From 1908 Rothesay Dock near Clydebank provided shipping facilities involving a shorter journey, and by the 1920s many Lanarkshire pits were worked out. There was still some profitable mineral traffic, notably to and from Glengarnock steelworks, but on the passenger side it was nearly all gloom for much of the L&A. Through services to Ardrossan Montgomerie Pier for the Arran and Isle of Man steamers had been fiercely contested by the G & SW, whilst local trains in Ayrshire were never much of a match for the opposition anyway. During 1932 the service from Glasgow Central was cut back to Uplawmoor and retreated further to Neilston in 1962. But further east Glasgow was spreading across the fields of Williamwood, Muirend, King's Park, Croftfoot and Burnside. So from the 1930s the L & A between Neilston and Newton became predominantly a passenger railway, complete with three new stations.

L & A stations with side platforms had attractive chalet–like buildings where the roof was extended to form a veranda, flanked by side screens. Whitecraigs was typical, although the high level goods station on Ayr Road was an unusual feature. This was the edge of the built up area and several services terminated here, but on 11th November 1955 Stanier 2–6–2 tank No.40176 was continuing to Neilston High with the 12.11 pm from Glasgow Central. Within a few minutes the train was crossing Waulkmill Glen Reservoir and in brighter weather passengers would have enjoyed a superb panorama from Clydebank to Carmyle with the Campsie Fells beyond. Whitecraigs had its own attraction in the form of Rouken Glen and before World War 1 there was a summer Sunday service of 10 trains for trippers.

Except for Ardrossan North, which had rambling half–timbered buildings and a flamboyant clock tower, L & A stations in Ayrshire were dull affairs. The Glasgow area fared much better however. Muirend was reminiscent of Cathcart Circle practice with its broad island platform and well–proportioned building featuring generous canopies. It had less ornamentation, although the Caledonian did provide a decorative entrance arch on Muirend Road bridge and a hint of 'Arts & Crafts' in the metal ventilation grill for the gents. There was also a large goods yards and ex–Caledonian Drummond 0–6–0 No.57244 shunted a couple of wagons into the shed on 8th November 1955. The yard closed in July 1965 and has since been redeveloped, but the passenger station survives virtually unaltered. Services improved dramatically with electrification and Muirend now has over 40 trains to Glasgow Central every weekday compared with 16 in 1955 and 12 in 1913.

Kirkhill on the Cathcart – Newton section had similar buildings to those at Whitecraigs, although they had canopies rather than verandas. It was also the terminus for certain short workings, and one of these was the 5.51 pm from Glasgow Central on 23rd May 1962. The start of electric services was less than a week away and Fairburn 2–6–4 tank No.42170 gave the overhead wire which heralded its demise a defiant blast of steam from the safety valves. East of Kirkhill the L & A had to tunnel through a low shoulder of the Cathkin Braes and beyond here a branch struck northwards to join the Newton – Carmyle line at Westburn Junction. Before World War 1 five out of the twelve trains from Glasgow Central to Kirkhill returned to Central this way, thus forming a circular service. Three went via Rutherglen to the main terminus and the other two were routed through Bridgeton Cross to Central Low Level. An early morning service from Kirkhill to Possil via Westburn Junction and Central Low Level was still running in 1953.

Municipal housing engulfing the L & A east of Cathcart justified new stations at King's Park and Croftfoot, which opened on 8th October 1928 and 1st April 1931 respectively. The former had a long island platform partly in a cutting and partly on an embankment reached by a ramp from Kingsbridge Drive and a subway from Aikenhead Road. The LMS building clearly had an affinity with its L & A and Cathcart Circle predecessors, but was cumbersome and squat by comparison. Yet, perhaps by chance, it blended quite well with the council houses on King's Park Avenue. Standard 5MT 4–6–0 No.73076, looking slightly uneasy working tender first, paused at King's Park with the 5.5 pm Glasgow Central – Kirkhill on 31st March 1961 as low cloud hung over the Cathkin Braes and a steady downpour drenched the estate.

Despite their lack of finesse, King's Park and Croftfoot were masterpieces compared with the other station built by the LMS to serve new housing developments near the L & A. Williamwood, between Muirend and Whitecraigs, opened on 9th July 1929 and consisted of wooden shacks with stovepipe chimneys. Platforms, lighting and fencing were a mishmash of timber and concrete, as seen here on 12th November 1955. The buildings were swept away and replaced by the present facilities in 1979. Originally this was the site of Clarkston West Junction, where the spur used by Caledonian coal trains during 1903 came in from the Busby Railway.

King's Park handled its share of football specials for big games at Hampden Park, although usually these came from outside the city and were generally fewer in number than those at Mount Florida just over half a mile away. The 1956 Scotland – England match for instance brought a total of six trains from Edinburgh, the Lanarkshire coalfield towns and Kilmarnock. Apart from a B1 on one of the Edinburgh trains, all were hauled by Stanier Black 5 4–6–0s. Empty stock of arrivals from the east was sent off to Muirend where two would stand in the goods yard and two or more on the never–connected spur to Clarkston East Junction. Others continued to Whitecraigs and even Neilston if necessary. Specials from the west were reversed into the loop sidings at King's Park or despatched to Newton.

L & A tracks formed a tangent with the Cathcart Circle at Cathcart, but did not actually run through the station. There were however connections at West and East Junctions which enabled trains from Glasgow Central via Queen's Park to reach Neilston and Newton. Although the section between the junctions had no regular passenger service it was used by football specials from Ayrshire to King's Park, and Black 5 No.45013 was getting into its stride as it stormed past Cathcart station with an excursion returning to Kilmarnock on 20th April 1957. Another special waited for the road into King's Park. On match days the late afternoon train from Uplawmoor to Glasgow Central was also diverted this way and provided an unofficial railtour. Instead of using the Inner Circle it travelled via Kirkhill, Westburn Junction, Carmyle and Rutherglen being allowed 30 minutes from Muirend to Central. With electrification the layout at Cathcart West Junction was altered to allow trains from the Inner Circle access to the Newton line – but still no platform was provided on the L & A route.

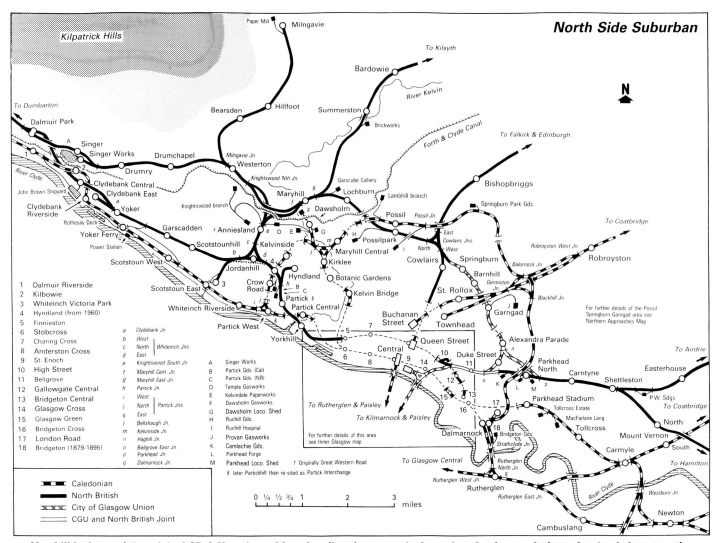

North Side Suburban

Maryhill had one of the original GD & H stations although at first there was single track and only one platform. Its simple but attractive brick building featured round–headed windows, stone relief and a glazed front to the waiting room and was still in reasonable condition on 8th April 1961 as class J37 0–6–0 No.64633 called with the 12.10 pm Saturday workers' service from Singer to Duke Street. Such trains were unadvertised and for several years prior to official closure on 2nd October 1961 the only call shown in the public timetable was an early morning Queen Street Low Level – Springburn – Milngavie working. Goods facilities survived until July 1969. The branch to Partick and Stobcross veered away to the left and this remained in use for freight until Maryhill signal box burnt down in October 1980.

Cast iron drinking fountain at Milngavie.

North British Suburban

The electric 'Blue Trains' have been synonymous with Glasgow suburban services for over thirty years. Although marred at the outset by a serious electrical fault which led to their withdrawal for eleven months, the introduction of these multiple units on the North Side in 1960 was probably the most dramatic change in rolling stock ever seen on a local BR network. The old order consisted of steam hauled non–corridor stock with watercolour prints on the partitions and leather straps to open the windows. The new trains had large saloons, with bright formica surfaces, four different seat trims and panoramic views. Furthermore the bulging contours, curved windscreens and very distinctive livery gave them a strong public image. As a result the whole of the former North British suburban system from Helensburgh to Airdrie had a unity as never before, despite the fact that a good measure of standardization had applied in the 1950s, when Gresley V1/V3 2–6–2 tanks had a virtual monopoly. The network selected

for electrification was not a worthy example of North British planning – instead it developed in a piecemeal fashion over a 30 year period. The Edinburgh & Glasgow tracks out of Queen Street were on their own for 16 years until a largely rural line, from Cowlairs to Dumbarton and Helensburgh, was completed in 1858. A variety of railways followed, including branches down to docks and shipyards on the Clyde, a secondary main line to Edinburgh and the City of Glasgow Union's north – south link. In 1886 this motley collection was fettled into a cohesive suburban system with the help of an underground route through the city centre. Nevertheless it was a complex arrangement and as late as 1951 the ex–North British lines still had no less than six termini within six miles of central Glasgow in addition to Queen Street. Now just one remains, although the system itself is largely intact. Indeed, with three classes of electric multiple units in use there is probably more variety at Queen Street Low Level than there has been for years.

GLASGOW DUMBARTON & HELENSBURGH

Two years after the Edinburgh & Glasgow was completed, local businessmen promoted a line from Cowlairs to Dumbarton, Balloch and Helensburgh along the north bank of the Clyde. Only the middle section of the Caledonian & Dumbartonshire Railway was built and trains began to run between Bowling and Balloch in 1850 with steamer connections from Glasgow. The full scheme was soon resurrected and the Glasgow, Dumbarton & Helensburgh Railway obtained its Act on 15th August 1855. It was opened as single track on 28th May 1858 utilising C & D metals from Bowling to Dumbarton. The GD & H was absorbed by the Edinburgh & Glasgow on 14th August 1862, which in turn became part of the North British three years later.

From a triangular junction at Cowlairs the line headed west through Possil, passed beneath the Forth & Clyde Canal at Lambhill, and crossed the Kelvin Valley on a nine arch viaduct north of Maryhill. Beyond here the GD & H paralleled the canal and ran through Kilbowie, Dalmuir and Old Kilpatrick on a generally falling gradient before reaching the shoreline at Bowling. In 1858 this was very much a rural transect and, indeed, the principal intention of the line was to encourage combined boat and train journeys between the Firth of Clyde, Loch Lomond and Glasgow. However, over the years it took on several new roles. Docks, factories and shipyards developed alongside the river and brought heavy freight traffic via feeder branches; long–distance residential services from Helensburgh flourished; and new stations such as Drumchapel, Westerton and Drumry opened at intervals to serve local needs. Although completion of the Queen Street Low Level line in 1886 had transformed the GD & H into a truly suburban route, when the West Highland line to Fort William opened in 1894 those trains heading for the mountains and moors beyond Helensburgh brought a touch of romance to the outskirts of Glasgow – a feeling still not entirely absent, despite the Sprinters.

Near Maryhill two branch lines joined the GD & H from the north. On 28th August 1863 the Glasgow & Milngavie Junction Railway opened 3¼ miles of single track from the little textile manufacturing town of Milngavie which nestled below the Kilpatrick Hills. At the time it might have appeared unpromising territory for a local passenger service, but the wealthy residential developments anticipated by the promoters soon occurred – particularly around the intermediate station at Bearsden. The G & MJ was absorbed by the North British in 1873 and a steady increase in passenger demand eventually led to the installation of double track and the opening of another station at Hillfoot, on 24th April and 1st May 1900 respectively. Electric trains began to run in 1960 and commuter traffic remains heavy. With a wooded backdrop to villas and golf links, and glimpses of distant hills, this is one of the most attractive stretches of suburban railway around Glasgow.

On 4th June 1879 the Kelvin Valley Railway finally completed its 11¼ mile line from Kilsyth to Maryhill, in the shadow of the Campsie Fells. The North British had treated the local company with a certain amount of disdain and an actual junction with the Helensburgh route was not installed until 1st October. New collieries in the valley and housing developments alongside the stations were eagerly awaited by the KV directors but nothing much happened, and the North British purchased the line for a bargain price in 1885. It was coal traffic from Twechar and Balmore Collieries to the Clyde docks that kept the line going, although the little used passenger services lingered on until 1951. Somewhat ironically the trackbed north of Maryhill is now flanked by houses and even obscured by them in places – far too late for the Kelvin Valley Railway.

North side suburban in transition. With the overhead wires in place and a new footbridge and platform edgings completed ready for electrification, V3 2–6–2T No.67648 pulled into Anniesland with the 2.26pm from Milngavie to Bridgeton Central on 6th June 1960.

Possilpark station dated from 1887, when the Queen Street Low Level circular service via Springburn, Maryhill and the West End commenced. Compared with the pleasing affair at Maryhill it was harsh and rather peculiar. The platform buildings were basically ugly yet had very decorative wooden canopies and absurdly ornate lamp brackets at each corner. Regular services ceased on 1st January 1917 but unadvertised workers trains continued and on 29th July 1959 there was still a solitary railwayman to greet the 5.22 pm Clydebank East – Springburn with 64633 in charge. Compartment doors on the newly outshopped articulated coaches at the front of the train were swinging open for a quick getaway. The long wall of tenements on Barnes Road and two remarkably tall signals controlling the Ruchill branch junction overlooked the scene. Withdrawal of goods facilities took place in July 1971. Presently only the running lines remain at Possil, but after an absence of nearly 80 years a passenger service to the city centre could soon return.

Four more stations were provided at the Glasgow end of the GD & H over the years. Drumchapel and Lochburn opened in 1890 to serve a nearby village and adjacent foundry respectively. Westerton was built in 1913 for a new 'garden suburb' and Drumry dates from 1953 when the nearby Corporation housing estates were being developed. Westerton still had its original plain timber buildings when a new 'Blue Train' performing driver training duties on the Milngavie branch reversed there on 22nd March 1960. In retrospect the tail lamp about to be placed on car SC75582 seems somewhat archaic on modern electric suburban stock.

Low evening sunlight picked out the train and exhaust alike as N2 0–6–2T No.69507 passed Milngavie Junction with the 4.33 pm from Dalmuir Park to Springburn, on 19th March 1958. Smoke from the hearths of Drumchapel hung in the cold air and blurred the distant Kilpatrick Hills.

Although Drumchapel station opened in 1890 for the benefit of the nearby village, it eventually served the housing scheme of the same name which sprawled over the lower slopes of the Kilpatrick Hills west of Bearsden. Gresley V1 2–6–2T No.67676 negotiated the reverse curve into Drumchapel on 16th May 1956 with the 11.0 am from Helensburgh Central to Bridgeton Central. From the early 1930s to electrification, the V1s and their more powerful V3 derivatives with higher boiler pressure had a virtual monopoly of suburban services over the former North British lines. They also worked local passenger trains in Edinburgh, Fife, Tyneside and East Anglia. The curved destination board in front of the V1's chimney had a pedigree dating back to North British days, but this particular one badly needed a clean. Electrification – which had been recommended by the 1955 Modernization Plan – led to the gradual demise of the boards, through the increasing danger from live overhead wires during testing.

On 13th July 1955 the dying sunlight of a glorious summer day picked out V3 2–6–2T No.67626 at Milngavie as its fire was being made up ready for the 9.10 pm departure to Airdrie. Despite electrification in 1960 and closure of the goods yard in September 1965, this delightful terminus has kept virtually all of its passenger facilities, including the original Glasgow & Milngavie Junction station building. In fact during an extensive rebuild of this listed structure in 1979 the flagstone floor of the ticket hall was retained and the clock, drinking fountain and elaborate 1899 canopy all carefully restored.

During the test running and driver training programme on the Milngavie branch there was a spate of 'Blue Train' failures and this led to the borrowing of green liveried Eastern Region 'Tilbury' sets – Nos.205, 258, 260 and 261 from July 1959 to January 1960. Set 205 paused at Bearsden in overcast conditions on 17th August 1959. The two storey Glasgow & Milngavie Junction station building at Bearsden was built of chiselled biscuit–coloured stone like Milngavie and it is now a restaurant.

Unadvertised passenger services over the Helensburgh line were largely generated by the huge Singer works at Clydebank which had its own terminus, consisting of three island platforms served by six tracks. The American sewing machine company opened its purpose–built factory next to Kilbowie station in 1883, eventually occupying over 100 acres and employing thousands of people from the Glasgow area. As the complex expanded it became necessary to divert ¾ mile of the GD & H line northwards and replace Kilbowie station (already renamed Singer) with new facilities on the deviation. This took effect on 3rd November 1907 and left a stub of the old route forming sidings into the factory, flanked by the works terminus, which handled up to fifteen trains each way at one time. There were still plenty of dedicated services to Bridgeton, Airdrie and the Springburn line on 26th August 1956, when 2–6–2Ts Nos.67648, 67625 and 67618, together with Ivatt Mogul No.43135, prepared for their respective departures. On the extreme left a D34 'Glen' 4–4–0 waited to back its train out of the platform before heading west to Dumbarton and Balloch. Rows of wagons occupied the original GD & H alignment and beyond them a bus crossed the 1907 route near the through station. Singer's bulbous clock tower peered through the steam and the Kilpatrick Hills overlooked the scene from a distance. All six tracks were electrified in 1960 but the mighty factory was doomed and the terminus closed in 1969. Although the name Singer survives as a Glasgow suburban station, Scotland's largest industrial site for many years has now been replaced by the Clydebank Shopping Centre.

The 1907 station at Singer was in the last stages of redecoration as V3 2–6–2T No.67628 rolled in with the 3.0 pm from Bridgeton Central to Helensburgh Central, on 8th October 1960, a month before the electrics took over. An electrification train putting finishing touches to the overhead wiring occupied the other track in the distance. The coach nearest the V1 was an ex–LMS non–corridor, illustrating the mixing up of suburban stock on the former LNER lines towards the end of steam. Singer's original buildings have now been swept away, as have the nearby tenements, though these have been replaced by new houses and flats.

STOBCROSS, WHITEINCH AND CLYDE-BANK

Despite burgeoning trade and larger ships, there was still a heavy dependence on the old Broomielaw quays near Glasgow Bridge in the mid–19th century. But by the 1860s increasing maritime congestion and lack of rail access to the north bank persuaded the Clyde Trustees to develop Queen's Dock on marshland a mile downstream at Stobcross. The Glasgow, Dumbarton & Helensburgh line was 2½ miles away to the north and authorisation for the necessary branch down to the river came in 1870.

The Stobcross Railway pursued a somewhat roundabout course, partly to take account of the contours, but also to avoid demolishing property in the growing suburbs of Maryhill, Kelvinside and Partick. Nevertheless, land acquisition proved an expensive business and several substantial bridges were required over existing streets. From Maryhill the new line ran due west, parallel to the Helensburgh route. It then passed under the Forth & Clyde Canal, turned southwards, and crossed Great Western Road near Anniesland. At Jordanhill the rails took up an easterly course, but soon veered south again through Partick. After a viaduct over the River Kelvin at Yorkhill the track split at Kelvinhaugh Junction, one branch serving a high level goods and mineral depot, the other descending steeply to the quayside.

Traffic to Queen's Dock commenced on 20th October 1874 and the Stobcross Railway immediately became an important North British goods artery. The Caledonian demanded running powers as well as joint ownership of the lines east of Kelvinhaugh Junction and these were reluctantly granted. Even after the commissioning of Rothesay Dock further down the river in 1907 there was plenty of work for the Stobcross quays, but eventually the decline of heavy industry in central Scotland deprived Queen's Dock of its traditional exports. After a period when the sidings and wharfs were more or less moribund, closure finally came in 1968. However, back in 1886 the Stobcross Railway had provided a convenient link with the Helensburgh line, when the underground route through Queen Street Low Level opened. New stations were built at Partick and Great Western Road, and a burrowing spur between Knightswood South and North Junctions opened on 1st August 1886, affording trains from central Glasgow direct access to the coast. Today, frequent Strathclyde electrics thread the curves through Partick and Anniesland with little to suggest the line has ever been other than a purely passenger railway.

The Whiteinch Railway opened along with the Stobcross line on 29th October 1874 and branched off it near Jordanhill. An enclave of small shipyards and factories grew up in open country alongside the Clyde at Whiteinch while Queen's Dock was taking shape two miles upstream, and the owners were eager to secure the advantages of rail transport for themselves. Goods traffic was handled by the North British as far as Dumbarton Road, but the associated tramway down to the river was privately operated. In 1891 the NB purchased the Whiteinch Railway and in view of the housing developments which had taken place nearby they inaugurated a passenger service on 1st January 1897. Victoria Park terminus continued to function as one of the more obscure backwaters of the Glasgow suburban network until 1951 and the branch survived for goods and departmental traffic until the late 1960s.

A far more successful riverside line was the Glasgow Yoker & Clydebank Railway, although it also originated from purely local needs. In the early 1870s J & G Thomson's shipyard was forced to relocate from Govan to a new site four miles away on the north bank. At the time this was a remote place devoid of housing and most workers still lived near the old yard. In association with Govan ferry and a nearby station at Partick on the Stobcross Railway, the GY & C was an attempt to provide the necessary link. Its single track from Jordanhill near the Whiteinch branch junction to a modest terminus, Clydebank East, close to the shipyard gates, opened on 1st December 1882. J & G Thomson became John Brown & Co. Ltd. and along with the Singer works transformed Clydebank into an important industrial town. The GY & C was converted to double track on 13th December 1896 and goods traffic commenced over a new extension to Dalmuir on 8th May 1897 followed by passenger services on 17th May. The company was acquired by the North British Railway on 15th July 1897. The old terminus was left at the end of a spur but was used by local trains and excursions until 1959. The through line was an instant success and never lost its importance; it was included in the electrification scheme of 1960 and is still a vital link today.

By 18th May 1955 the broad platform at Summerston was gradually reverting to nature and epitomized the misguided optimism of the Kelvin Valley Railway. Although Maryhill was less than two miles away behind the distant slopes of Cawder Cuilt, Summerston remained a hamlet and its primitive weatherboarded waiting room still stood in open marshy country. Here the line had its sole encounter with the River Kelvin which was spanned by the bowstring girder bridge in the distance. The sparse passenger service between Kilsyth and Queen Street Low Level via Torrance and Maryhill finished on 2nd April 1951 but unstaffed public goods facilities remained. In reality this amounted to a siding where coal from three or four mineral wagons was bagged by local merchants; meanwhile traffic from Blackhill Brickworks in the background was transferred to road transport. New diesel multiple units on driver training duties used the line in 1958, but through freight was eventually withdrawn and Summerston yard expired in July 1961.

For nearly twelve years after its opening in October 1874 most of the Stobcross branch carried only goods traffic, but March 1886 saw the start of the intensive suburban passenger service which has continued for over a century. Anniesland station – called Great Western Road until January 1931 – dates from that time and on 2nd July 1958 V1 2–6–2T No.67623 rolled in with the 5.26 pm from Springburn to Balloch Central. The bowstring lattice girder bridge was erected in about 1930 when Great Western Road was widened and it still stands, having been retained during electrification.

Partick station, renamed Partickhill in the early 1950s, was always one of the busiest on the North British suburban network and in 1914 had 14 trains to the city centre in just 54 minutes during the morning peak. Until early BR days it even advertised itself as 'for Govan' (via the Underground). But on 26th September 1960 thoughts were far from work as a very well patronised Glasgow autumn holiday excursion from Balloch to Edinburgh Waverley via Singer, Queen Street Low Level and Springburn called with B1 4–6–0s Nos.61099 and 61081 in charge. Modular wooden buildings dating from 1886 were replaced by BR reinforced concrete and brick in the 1950s, which in turn succumbed to the curved brown glass and escalators of Partick Interchange, 200 yards south on 17th December 1979. The old station survives, with the main building in use as offices. Somewhat remarkably, both the North British and Caledonian goods depots behind the station remained in use until July 1979. The latter dated from 1876 and was isolated from its owner's metals for nearly twenty years until a reverse shunt was installed from nearby Crow Road, on the new Lanarkshire & Dumbartonshire line.

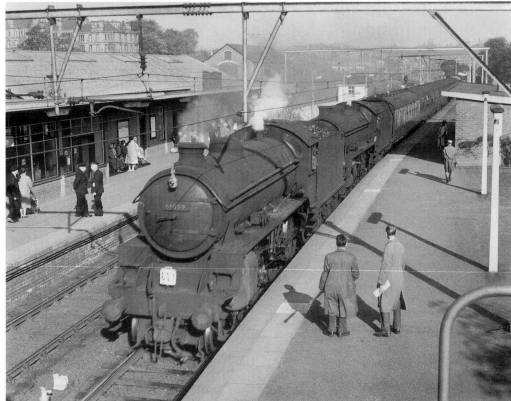

Engines manufactured by the North British Locomotive Company found their way all over the world and most of them were shipped from Queen's Dock. East African Railways 2–8–2 No.2927 stood at Stobcross Quay awaiting shipment to Mombasa, Kenya, on 4th December 1954. Derived from the Nigerian Railways 'Rivers', the 31 EAR 'Tribal' class locos were built by NBL from 1951 to 1955 and No.2927 was named SUK on entering service. By the late 1970s EAR was fully dieselised and SUK had become redundant. Meanwhile its birthplace had been demolished and Queens Dock was being transformed into the unprepossessing Scottish Exhibition and Conference Centre. But the giant Finnieston Crane which hoisted locomotives destined for export aboard their allotted ships is still a powerful reminder of the one–time global demand for Glasgow–built locomotives.

A sprinkling of snow lingered at Whiteinch Victoria Park on 23rd February 1956 as K2 2–6–0 No.61769 shunted the yard. The view from Danes Drive bridge showed an unmistakably urban setting, but it was all fields and hedgerows when the Whiteinch Railway and its associated tramway down to the river opened in 1874. On the left stood the 1897 passenger terminus – an island platform and narrow uninspiring timber buildings with a huge canopy, typical of contemporary North British practice. There were never more than a dozen daily services in or out, all via Queen Street Low Level. Passenger services ceased on 2nd April 1951. The tramway ran along Scotstoun Street, identified by the gap in the Dumbarton Road tenements in the background. General goods traffic at Victoria Park ceased in May 1965 but most of the branch stabled electrification maintenance trains, until February 1967.

The terminus of the Glasgow, Yoker & Clydebank Railway featured a narrow island platform, an exceedingly plain two storey house and a single storey block with classical embellishments. It was raining steadily on 18th July 1959 – seemingly inevitable weather for Glasgow Fair – as Parkhead B1 4–6–0 No.61333 prepared to leave Clydebank East with the 9.45 am special for Whitley Bay. Meanwhile, on the Dalmuir extension to the right, V3 2–6–2T No.67679 drew away from Clydebank Central in charge of the 9.5 am Helensburgh – Bridgeton Central. Other Fair specials that day were Clydebank East – Anstruther, Dalmuir Riverside – Aberdeen, Dumbarton – Dunbar, Springburn – Blackpool, and Airdrie – St. Andrews. As a prelude to electrification, Clydebank East closed for both passenger and goods traffic on 14th September 1959.

John Brown's shipyard at Clydebank, where some of the world's mightiest ocean liners took shape, relied heavily on rail for transporting both its raw materials and workers. But the great days were almost over by 26th February 1958, when the company's vintage pug – locally manufactured by Neilson in 1896 – ground across the tram tracks of Dumbarton Road with plate wagons from Clydebank West goods. Rail access ended about 1978 by which time the shipyard was under new ownership and had gone over to building oil rigs.

After negotiating Saltmarket and High Street Junctions, A2 Pacific No.60519 HONEYWAY eased through Bellgrove with the 8.15 pm 'Starlight Special' from St. Enoch to London Marylebone via Edinburgh Waverley on 25th May 1956. The 'Starlights' operated via Edinburgh off–peak and usually went through Springburn and along the E & G main line, but others occasionally travelled through Coatbridge. At the London end, use was made of the Great Central line to avoid congestion at St. Pancras or Kings Cross. Glasgow's huge cattle market spanned the tracks west of Bellgrove station and before the switch to road transport, trains from distant railheads such as Brechin and Dunbar arrived overnight for the Wednesday auctions. Livestock traffic finally ceased in July 1967.

Parkhead motive power depot (65C) was about a mile east of Bellgrove and it worked passenger services over the whole of the North British suburban system in Glasgow, as well as trains to Edinburgh via Bathgate until 1956. Goods duties included shunting High Street and Port Dundas together with trips to Govan, Paisley and Johnstone. In the mid–1950s about 70 engines were shedded here. A typical passenger allocation comprised a couple of dozen V1/V3 2–6–2Ts and 8 or so N2 0–6–2Ts for suburban work, a few B1 4–6–0s and K2 Moguls for longer distances and a couple of ageing North British C16 4–4–2Ts as station pilots. Ex–North British J35/36/37 0–6–0s and N15 0–6–2Ts made up the balance on the freight side. With electrification and the decline in goods traffic about to make them superfluous, V1 67678 and J37 64561 awaited their next duties at Parkhead, on 29th July 1960.

Most stations on the Glasgow & Coatbridge line were fairly rudimentary, but Parkhead North with its stone waiting room, brick office building and wooden goods cabin was a bit of a hotchpotch as well. Even the suffix 'North', acquired in June 1952, was tacked below the nameboard as an afterthought. The station is seen here on 30th August 1955, looking east towards Parkhead Junction where traffic from Cowlairs via Haghill Junction came in. Across nearby Duke Street was the mighty Parkhead Forge which shrouded its surroundings in smoke by day and lit them up with columns of fire by night. But with few houses in the immediate vicinity and three other stations close by, Parkhead North lost its passenger services on 19th September 1955, although the goods yard survived until October 1966. Eventually the ironworks followed suit and the giant steam hammers which had shaken Parkhead fell silent. Part of the site is now occupied by the Forge Shopping Centre and there is talk of a new station to serve it.

College station – one of the most ornate and certainly the oldest station building in Glasgow.

GLASGOW & COATBRIDGE

So the North British suburban system west of Glasgow city centre emerged from a series of local lines associated with the River Clyde in one way or another. But in the east end it was a secondary main line which formed the basis of the network. A branch from Edinburgh to Bathgate dating from 1849 was extended as far as Coatbridge in 1862 and it seemed logical to push this through to Glasgow, thus forming an alternative to the existing Edinburgh & Glasgow route. The Glasgow & Coatbridge Railway was authorised in 1865 and proved to be one of the last promotions by the Edinburgh & Glasgow company before it was absorbed by the North British.

The approach to Glasgow through Easterhouse, Shettleston and Carntyne was straightforward enough, but beyond Parkhead the line was entangled both physically and legally with the City of Glasgow Union Railway which had obtained its Act the previous year. The CGU (see next section for details) on its way from Shields Road south of the river, to Springburn in the north, intercepted the Coatbridge line near its terminus on High Street. As a result there was a half mile stretch of track through Bellgrove under communal ownership, with the CGU from Shields Road trailing in at Sydney Street Junction (now High Street Junction) and leaving for Springburn at Bellgrove Junction. The Glasgow & Coatbridge terminus stood about 700 yards west of Sydney Street Junction and was named College in recognition of the University of Glasgow which previously occupied the site. Indeed one of the university's ornate medieval buildings became the station entrance and offices. But behind this noble facade the facilities were penny-pinching to say the least, and few regretted their demotion to goods sidings 15 years later, when construction of the Queen Street low level line required a new through station.

Pending the completion of its College terminus, the North British ran a limited service from Coatbridge to Gallowgate on the CGU – just beyond Sydney Street Junction. This began on 19th December 1870. Edinburgh Waverley – Glasgow College trains commenced on 1st April 1871, but they were never very fast and most through passengers continued to use the original route via Falkirk. After the Queen Street low level line opened in 1886 suburban traffic became increasingly important on the Coatbridge line, although the Edinburgh service managed to survive until 9th January 1956.

On 1st November 1877 Shettleston became a junction when the western arm of the amply-named Glasgow, Bothwell, Hamilton & Coatbridge Railway opened for mineral traffic. The company had been formed by Lanarkshire ironmasters in 1874, principally to carry coal from the Bothwell area to their Coatbridge furnaces, although the North British provided discreet but heavy backing as a way of probing Caledonian territory. A Hamilton – College passenger service began on 1st April 1878, the GBH & C was absorbed by the North British in 1879, and the line continued to carry coal until the last colliery served by it closed in 1949. Passenger trains to Glasgow continued until 1955.

Bellgrove was the first stop out of College on the Coatbridge line, but it was also on the City Union, which gave some importance to what would otherwise have been an ordinary east end station. Firstly, Glasgow & South Western 'bus trains' from Shields Road started on 1st June 1871, providing connections with the Edinburgh service. Then on 1st September 1872 through coaches between Edinburgh and Ayr commenced with the transfer taking place at Bellgrove. The Ayrshire link finished on 30th September 1899 and the 'bus trains' on 1st October 1902, but by this time Bellgrove was on the Queen Street low level route anyway. Standard tram No.880 bound for Bellahouston near the old haunts of the long-vanished G & SW service headed along Bellgrove Street on 12th June 1958. The ample but uninspiring North British building behind it was destroyed by a malicious fire on 21st September 1980.

Carntyne was considerably neater than Parkhead and its timber buildings with their steeply–pitched roofs and glazed side screens could even be described as charming. The station retained its Victorian character, albeit decaying, as V3 2–6–2T No.67611 drifted in with a varied set of coaches forming the 11.35 am Hyndland to Easterhouse on 7th May 1956. Both Carntyne and Easterhouse three miles down the line were tiny places when the railway was built. The former became a garden suburb in the 1930s whereas the latter developed into one of Glasgow Corporation's more notorious housing estates during the 1950s. For a while some trains terminated at Easterhouse specifically for the housing scheme, but such short workings increased because of electrification construction work.

Shettleston had a rather poverty stricken brick building facing the approach from Annick Street. It was in keeping with the industrial background but somewhat shamed by the very fine tenements of Balgair Terrace on the opposite side of the tracks. On 20th April 1957 B1 4–6–0 No.61404 started off from Shettleston with the 10 am special from Bellgrove to Edinburgh Waverley. It just happened to be a Haymarket engine returning home from earlier duties which hauled this Easter excursion from the east end to the capital. Another special to call at Shettleston that day was from Airdrie to Largs (B1 No.61140) and BR had announced that it was the largest programme of excursions from Glasgow suburban stations since the war.

Mount Vernon North was the first station out of Shettleston on the former Glasgow, Bothwell, Hamilton & Coatbridge Railway and it was even more basic than those built for the main line. As with Carntyne this was a sparsely populated area at first, but in late Victorian times middle class villas began to colonise the sandy slopes near the station. By the 1930s Mount Vernon had become a residential suburb. There was still a reasonable service of 11 trains each way on weekdays and 8 on Saturdays when N2 0–6–2T No.69510 arrived with the 2.38 pm from Bothwell to Hyndland on 2nd July 1955. This sunny afternoon saw the last passenger trains at Mount Vernon North, the official closure date being 4th July. Goods was handled at the station until October 1965 but with the working out of the Lanarkshire coalfield the branch as a whole saw little other than commuter traffic in its last years.

CITY OF GLASGOW UNION

As described earlier in the Southern Approaches chapter, the City of Glasgow Union was a joint venture by the Glasgow & South Western and Edinburgh & Glasgow companies. Its line from West Street Junction on the Glasgow & Paisley Joint to the Sighthill goods branch at Springburn was authorised on 29th July 1864 and a year later the North British entered the partnership, having absorbed the Edinburgh & Glasgow. Priority was given to the southern half with its land acquisition difficulties and costly viaducts. As a result the Bellgrove – Springburn section did not open until 16th August 1875, nearly five years after the rest of the line, and then only for goods traffic.

However, this part of the CGU also involved some substantial engineering work. For over a mile beyond Bellgrove Junction there was a severe climb, largely through a succession of cuttings spanned by numerous road over–bridges. Short tunnels were necessary at Duke Street, under the Monkland Canal north of Alexandra Park, and near Blochairn Iron works on the approach to Garngad. As the gradient eased a further tunnel was required under the Garnkirk & Glasgow embankment, the adjacent Buchanan Street line, and some of the Sighthill goods tracks.

Establishing passenger services was an even more sluggish process than building the line. G & SW 'bus trains' were extended from Bellgrove to new stations at Duke Street and Alexandra Park (later renamed Alexandra Parade) on 1st January 1881, then to Garngad and Barnhill on 1st October 1883. Springburn station was brought into use on 1st January 1887, followed by the North British 'circular' service via Queen Street Low Level, the CGU, and Maryhill on 1st February. Despite the initial indifference to passenger traffic, this section of the CGU soon became very heavily used for journeys to and from work. Many people from the crowded east end were employed by the shipyards of Clydebank and Govan, the mills and factories of Paisley and Renfrew, and most of all by the Singer works. An intense railway operation developed to cope with the morning exodus and evening return, although this was partially offset by the daily influx to the North British Locomotive works at Springburn.

When the CGU was dissolved on 7th August 1896 and split up between its partners, the Bellgrove – Springburn section became part of the North British Railway. Glasgow & South Western goods workings to Springburn continued and so did the 'bus trains', but these were suffering increasingly from tramway competition and the service was getting a reputation for unreliability. It finished on 1st October 1902 except for workers trains from Springburn to Govan and Renfrew. The North British cut back its 'circular' operations on 12th January 1903 making Springburn virtually a terminus, although again there were unadvertised services from the Cowlairs direction, notably the Singer trains. Another casualty was Garngad station on 1st March 1910. This particular area had more industry than housing and the limited business that did exist easily fell prey to the trams along Royston Road. The other four stations closed to normal traffic in January 1917 as a wartime economy measure, but after they reopened in June 1919 little changed for 40 years. Electrification as far as Springburn came in 1960, but the workers' specials perished shortly afterwards and the CGU stations are a lot quieter now, even at peak times. They still enjoy a half hourly service throughout the day however.

The tightly–packed East End districts of Dennistoun, Haghill and Camlachie met at Duke Street station making this one of the busiest places on the line in its heyday. As Coronation and Standard trams passed the grimy four-storey tenements of Duke Street itself, V1 2–6–2T No.67629 emerged from the tunnel under Millerston Street with the 5.32 pm Clydebank East to Springburn on 21st May 1959. The 1 in 70 climb from Bellgrove meant that engines had to work hard with a heavy train like this, and the driver had only just eased off the regulator. Economy was clearly a major consideration in the design of the platform buildings.

On Duke Street itself the City Union put up a bleak little building in a stark classical style. Square columns with square capitals flanked doors and windows, a severe cornice formed the roofline and a vaguely Egyptian decoration was a strange touch at eye level. On 5th March 1960 part of it was occupied by Elspeth Fashions (phone number BR1 2960 when there were not that many telephones in Bridgeton!) who were showing off the latest lingerie. Alongside, a poster advertised a film at the nearby Odeon starring Gina Lollobrigida. Standard car No.556 headed west along Duke Street bound for Scotstoun West, a short working of route 1 from Dalmarnock to Dalmuir. The trams were replaced by bus service 58 a week later.

With no let up in the gradient it was a short sharp slog over the ¼ mile stretch from Duke Street to Alexandra Parade and V3 2–6–2T No.67626, with eight coaches in tow, was making its presence known at Haghill Junction on 28th May 1958. The train was the 5.32 pm Clydebank East – Springburn again. Authorised in 1873 and opened with the main line, the Haghill Junction to Parkhead spur permitted through freight workings between Cowlairs and Coatbridge. It never carried a regular passenger service and was taken out of use on 10th August 1981. Haghill Yard in the background was shared by the civil engineers and a number of coal merchants at the time of the photograph. It closed as a public depot in October 1965, though some permanent way sidings continued for a while.

Alexandra Park station was renamed Alexandra Parade by the LNER in July 1923 to distinguish it from one in Manchester they had just inherited from the Great Central Railway. In Glasgow both suffixes were appropriate, for the nearby streets of Milnbank were a comparatively elegant enclave between the working class east end and industrial Garngad. Bay windows and even a little turret were evident in Bannatyne Avenue and Alexandra Park Street as V1 2–6–2T No.67623 drifted in with the 5.15 pm Hyndland to Springburn on 28th May 1958.

Garngad station, remote from dense housing and surrounded by sidings, was already in trouble when the tramways were electrified and it closed to passengers as early as 1st March 1910. The afternoon of Sunday 26th April 1959 was damp and dismal, but Stanier 5MT 4–6–0 No.45174 brought a spark of interest as it passed the site of Garngad's platforms with the 9.40 am from Aberdeen to Glasgow Queen Street. This diversion was because Buchanan Street was closed on winter Sundays and engineers had possession of the line to Queen Street main line station. A bleak panorama was revealed from Royston Road bridge, stretching from the Garngad goods yard tracks on the left to a disused connection to Provan Gasworks on the extreme right. St. Rollox high bank, created by the Garnkirk & Glasgow Railway, formed a horizontal skyline, largely occupied by coaches and wagons awaiting attention in St. Rollox Works.

Several industrial establishments were linked to the CGU and the large number of sidings at Garngad were to deal with mineral traffic at two of the most important sites. To the south a branch led off to Blochairn Ironworks whilst on the north side a line curved sharply away towards Glasgow Corporation's Provan Gasworks. The latter occupied a huge area and for a long time was the city's principal supplier of street lighting. Until 1958 it had its own 2ft. 6in. gauge internal railway for servicing the retorts, where coal was converted into town gas and coke. Very limited clearances meant that the ten diminutive engines looked as if they belonged at a seaside pleasure park, but in reality they worked hard in a hot and hostile environment. Dalmarnock, Dawsholm and Tradeston gasworks had similar 2ft. 0in. gauge systems. Provan's 0–4–0 No.4 propelled a hopper wagon towards the retorts on 5th June 1954. One of these locomotives is preserved on the Welshpool & Llanfair Light Railway.

By the time it reached Springburn the CGU was running parallel to the Sighthill branch and had already made a connection with it near Barnhill. Springburn station itself had ordinary through platforms, but also gained a couple of bays on the east side, when it was decided to terminate most trains there. At street level the sizeable booking office once again demonstrated the severe architectural style adopted by CGU engineer G.Carsewell. Coronation tram No.1186 passed the building as it approached the end of route 16 on 21st August 1959. This particular structure has gone, but a station house in the same style survives. Also no more are the mighty Atlas and Hydepark works of the North British Locomotive Company, which flanked the track between Barnhill and Springburn stations. The factories closed in 1963 and were demolished about six years later.

Beyond Springburn the CGU curved round towards the Edinburgh & Glasgow main line at Cowlairs and on the evening of 28th July 1960 J37 0–6–0 No.64639 ambled south along this section with a Singer to Duke Street workers' service. The double track Sighthill goods branch ran alongside the CGU and separated it from the sidings known unofficially as the Turkey Yard. This curious name recalled the prolific traffic from the United Turkey Red Company which once passed through the sidings. The firm had a works at Alexandria near Dumbarton and enjoyed a virtual monopoly of Turkey Red dye before World War 1. Most of the remaining tracks were lifted in 1991 to make way for the new Cowlairs curve. Prominent on the hillside are the baronial–style tenements, built by the Edinburgh & Glasgow Railway for its workers. Known as 'the blocks', they formed several terraces off Fernbank Street but have now been demolished.

GLASGOW CITY & DISTRICT

By the early 1880s there was a pressing need for better communications from the east end to shipyards, docks and factories on the north bank and between the west end and central Glasgow. The North British already had a network of sorts throughout the North Side, but in reality it was a collection of branches with little co–ordination between them. Furthermore, Queen Street was seriously congested, College was inconvenient, and certain lines were devoid of passenger services anyway. A 1¼ mile branch from Stobcross to a terminus at the corner of Hope Street and Bothwell Street, for local traffic from the west was considered, until a shareholder suggested that this would encourage through passengers to use the Caledonian's new Central station opposite. It merely nibbled at the problem anyway and the North British realised that the Glasgow suburban nettle would have to be grasped firmly, thus the very expensive but extremely useful line below the city centre.

The Glasgow City & District Railway was authorised in 1882. Its 2¼ mile route from Stobcross through Finnieston, Charing Cross and Queen Street Low Level to the Coatbridge line near College involved 1¾ miles of tunnelling. Work began in March 1883 with only the Metropolitan and Metropolitan District in London and the Mersey Railway in Liverpool offering guidelines for urban underground construction. 'Cut and cover' was used as much as possible, but shafts were often necessary and at one stage excavation was taking place at more than 20 sites. Geological conditions presented problems and some innovative engineering work was required. Fortunately much of the tunnelling took place in free–splitting sandstone, which could be used for retaining walls and other structural work elsewhere. But

there was usually a cover of boulder clay, difficult to blast when dry yet a slithering mass when wet. East of Queen Street a firm footing lay well below track level, so brick piers were sunk, in effect forming a deeply buried viaduct supporting the tunnel. Considerable care was taken to minimise disruption above the course of the railway. Tram lines were underpinned overnight in time for the resumption of services, blasting was meticulously controlled and several buildings had to be shored up, although inevitably some property was demolished. Making room for Queen Street Low Level station was an enormous project. It took two years of patient digging because the overworked terminus above was vitally important to the North British and undue interference with its operation had to be avoided. As a result material was removed in a succession of strips so that only one main line track at a time was out of use.

The most frustrating conditions emerged when engineers attempted to use the 'cut & cover' technique along Kent Road, between Finnieston and Charing Cross. They encountered waterlogged sand which shifted alarmingly and the neighbouring tenements threatened to join the navvies in the trench! Consequently, metal piles were installed either side of the street and sufficient sand was removed so that a concrete roof could be built. Cavities were then gently excavated while water was syphoned off into drains and more concrete was poured into the troughs to form the tunnel walls. With the dwellings of Kent Road secured, sand was removed from within this rigid shell. But a large sewer along the length of the street presented another problem and section by section it had to be diverted into new pipes clear of the tunnel.

Eventually the GC & D was ready and passenger services began, on 15th March 1886.

The scope for a comprehensive North Side suburban service was enormous, although several months elapsed before this was fully implemented, pending the completion of new lines and stations elsewhere. A spur between Great Western Road and Knightswood North Junction, opened on 1st August 1886, was particularly significant as it allowed direct running from Queen Street Low Level to Dumbarton, Balloch and Helensburgh. College terminus was replaced by through platforms at a lower level (renamed High Street on 1st January 1914) and the old station was absorbed into the Glasgow & South Western's College goods depot. The GC & D officially passed into North British ownership during 1887 after being controlled and worked by them from the outset.

Two short branches were spawned by the underground line. Each provided a convenient terminus for suburban services from the opposite side of the city and both had space for several carriage sidings. Hyndland was a developing middle class suburb popular with city businessmen when a half mile branch from Partick Junction on the Stobcross line opened on 15th March 1886. At one stage the North British considered taking it as far as Botanic Gardens, but the line that opened on the same day as the GC & D ended at Hyndland Road. Bridgeton in the east end was in danger of becoming a Caledonian monopoly, so the North British opened a ¾ mile branch on 1st June 1892. From a burrowing junction at College it passed below the cramped Calton district in a series of tunnels and stone–walled cuttings. There was an intermediate station at Gallowgate Central and from 1893 to 1913 more passenger trains came in there, over a spur from the City Union. However a St. Enoch – Bridgeton service must have been of dubious value even in late Victorian times.

From its junction with the Stobcross branch high above the docks, the GC&D descended rapidly and went underground at Argyle Street. This was the site of Finnieston station which had a long single storey entrance block of somewhat harsh appearance facing the road. It looked permanent enough, but the public opted for the trams. By 1914 no trains were stopping at Finnieston after 6pm and the station closed on 1st January 1917 as a wartime cost–saving measure, never to re–open. Nevertheless the building survived until destroyed by fire in1993.

Charing Cross station at the other end of Kent Road was a better investment than Finnieston. For years it served the fashionable shops of Sauchiehall Street, a wealthy residential area, and the popular King's Theatre. Although the west end of the city centre has changed there is still a steady flow of traffic. There was some criticism when a fine Georgian crescent was demolished to make way for the station, but this was nothing compared with the attacks from Glasgow Corporation once the line was built. The 'scandalous' conditions at Charing Cross were an easy target. Both approaches were on rising gradients and trains pushed clouds of smoke from the tunnels. When the North British planned to open up a ventilation shaft some way towards Queen Street the council would not allow it and part of the roof at Charing Cross was removed as a compromise. But a certain amount of smoke persisted and V1 2–6–2T No.67618 added to the haze on 2nd July 1958 as it rolled in through the sunshine and shadows with the 4.42 pm from Balloch to Shettleston. The street level building was similar to that at Finnieston, but it was demolished when the M8 motorway was built.

Although the bulk of Queen Street Low Level was under a massive girder roof, there were gaps in front of the tunnel mouths, each containing a signal cabin perched above the tracks. But ventilation remained poor and with its very intensive service the station was usually a dark and smoky cavern. In 1914 there were about 165 trains each way on weekdays, varying from the Craigendoran boat express to a few true circle workings from Maryhill back to Maryhill, which ceased on 1st January 1917. New Reid 4–4–2T had displaced the old Drummond 0–4–4s and 4–4–0s used since the line was built, but the rough–riding four and six wheel coaches still had a few years to run. By 1958 Low Level was displaying an even thicker veneer of soot and Gresley V1/V3 2–6–2Ts hauling LNER bogie compartment stock had been the norm for years. There were 98 trains in each direction between 5.25 am and 11 pm including the 8.25 am business express from Helensburgh, nicknamed the 'Bowler Hat', which took just 44 minutes. Overtaking was always a feature of the station and as late as 1958 the 5.28 pm Clydebank East – Airdrie waited for 14 minutes while the 5.24 pm Milngavie – Bridgeton and 5.32 pm Clydebank East – Springburn passed. In the days when a trilby hat and belted raincoat were standard commuting wear, V1 2–6–2T No.67632 prepared to leave Queen Street Low Level with the 4.52 pm Airdrie to Hyndland on 8th May 1959.

Rather than being numbered, the low level platforms at Queen Street were lettered A, B, C and D until 1954, when a new indicator board was erected in the high level station to replace the original structure, demolished on 3rd March of that year by a banker bringing in empty stock for the 'Queen of Scots' Pullman. The low level then became platforms 10 to 13, thus creating one station as far as the public were concerned. During August 1959 the underground part was completely remodelled as a prelude to electrification. The eastbound platforms were closed and new connections installed so that Airdrie, Bridgeton and Springburn trains could use one of the tracks previously employed for westbound services. Accumulated grime was also removed and walls were resurfaced with new tiling. The full electric service began on 7th November 1960 but a spate of switchgear explosions – one of which seriously injured a guard – meant that steam had to come to the rescue on 19th December. At the east end of Queen Street Low Level on 23rd June 1961 V1 2–6–2T No.67608 rushed in with the 4.14 pm Bridgeton Central – Dalmuir Park, as sister V1 No.67681 waited to leave with the 3.59 pm Garscadden – Airdrie. Ironically, Garscadden was a new station built specially for the electric service. The 'Blue Trains' finally returned on 1st October 1961.

At Hyndland the North British put up a surprisingly grand building, harking back to the 'Railway Italianate' of the 1840s, but an appropriate style in view of the fine terraces of Great Western Road just round the corner. The tall two storey block had a projecting central section with a triangular pediment and symmetrical wings featuring a pronounced cornice and parapet. Clearly the architect wanted a variety of windows – triangular and segmental pediments on the first floor, plain headers for the ground floor wings, and a large semi–circular fanlight to emphasise the entrance. But the elegant terminus was soot–blackened and doomed as Standard trams Nos.224 and 488 waited at the end of route 10 from London Road on 16th January 1960. They had even less time left than the station, for the service was withdrawn within five months.

Behind the noble facade at Hyndland, and down a flight of stairs, was a lengthy island platform, sheltered at its inner end by an iron and glass canopy. There were also several carriage sidings to the north and a small turntable and locomotive water tower near the buffer stops. Most passenger services were purely local in character. In 1914 there were 30 trains each way, mainly to and from Airdrie and Hamilton but including two departures for Edinburgh via Bathgate and four return workings. These through trains, inherited from the old College terminus, took about 2¼ hours and consisted of four–wheelers hauled by ageing Wheatley 4–4–0s. A few years before there had even been two through coaches from London, bearing 'Kings Cross – Glasgow (Hyndland)' boards and conveyed by the 11.20 am summer express. Scott, Glen and Director 4–4–0s eventually dominated the Edinburgh service and latterly it was worked by B1 4–6–0s until withdrawn in 1956. By 1958 there were 15 trains each way, including return workings to Kirkintilloch, Shettleston and Easterhouse. Somewhat earlier, on 16th August 1954, V3 2–6–2T No.67662 waited to leave Hyndland with the 11.35 am to Shettleston, as smartly turned–out Parkhead N2 0–6–2T No.69565 looked on.

The small coal yard at Hyndland, served by an occasional trip working, closed in May 1958 – but far greater changes were in store with electrification. A large rolling stock maintenance shed with three inspection pit roads, each capable of taking a 6–car set, was erected on the site of the carriage sidings. Meanwhile a new through station to replace the terminus was taking shape less than half a mile away. Towards the end, V1 2–6–2T No.67633 stood at Hyndland with the 5.22 pm departure for Airdrie on 15th July 1960, as brand new 'Blue Trains' waited to make their debut. The last passenger services over the branch were on 5th November 1960 and the grand station building was subsequently demolished. Eventually even Hyndland electric depot yielded to the march of progress, for it closed on 23rd June 1987 when the new facilities at Yoker took over its work. The branch was lifted early in 1988 and houses now occupy the site of the terminus.

Compared with Hyndland, the terminus erected at Bridgeton Cross six years later was an ungainly edifice. Its ground floor arcade, repetitive upper storey windows, projecting ends and heavy cornice formed an oddly–proportioned facade which sat confidently but discordantly amid the tenements of London Road. On 13th April 1961 Bridgeton Central, as it had become, displayed the new electrification logo, consisting of a yellow arrow representing a pantograph superimposed on a blue arrow representing the Clyde estuary. Not that any 'Blue Trains' were working at the time, for steam had made its temporary comeback. Standard car No.76 was running above the Caledonian underground line, which was doomed as a result of the North British electrification – yet the subterranean route ultimately triumphed when its re-instatement rendered the terminus superfluous. The main building still exists and is currently in use as – a betting shop.

Bridgeton was an impressive terminus and had a timetable to match. In 1914 there were about 60 arrivals and the same number of departures, mainly Helensburgh and Balloch trains, plus unadvertised workers' services for Singer, Govan and Renfrew. During the 1950s the east end also had a Sunday service to Loch Lomond and the Clyde Coast and even a summer excursion to Fort William. On Sunday 10th July 1955 V1 2–6–2T No.67643 waited with the 5.45 pm to Helensburgh, while classmate No.67678 stood on the far side with empty stock. Bridgeton Central closed on 5th November 1979 when nearby Bridgeton Cross on the Argyle line reopened. Apart from loco coal there was no goods. Like Hyndland the terminus had been a carriage depot from the outset and went on to house the 'Blue Trains'. It also fell victim to Yoker and closed on 1st June 1987.

Viewed from Gallowgate bridge, V1 2–6–2T No.67622 led the 4.8 pm Milngavie – Bridgeton Central through the massive stone–faced cutting between Barnack Street and Sydney Street, on 9th August 1956. This was the site of Bridgeton Cross South Junction where the Glasgow & South Western spur from St. Johns came in through the tunnel on the left. A Bellahouston – Bridgeton Cross passenger service began on 1st April 1893, but it was cut back to St. Enoch – Bridgeton Cross in 1897 and withdrawn altogether in 1898 except for a few unadvertised workmens' trains, which ceased on 1st February 1913. The tunnel was then blocked up and served as a railway employees' rifle range for a while. Dingy Gallowgate Central station was in the equally deep cutting behind the camera on the opposite side of the road. It closed on 1st January 1917 but the moderately grand street level building survived until the early 1980s having had a spell as a sausage skin factory.

The first station out of Stobcross was Partick Central which stood on a stone–faced embankment built up from the rocky bed of the River Kelvin. On 15th June 1959 it was renamed Kelvin Hall as a prelude to the Scottish Industries Exhibition in the nearby centre of the same name. Three months later, on 19th September, a six coach exhibition special from Edinburgh Princes Street arrived at the island platform behind preserved Caledonian 4–2–2 No.123 and Great North of Scotland Railway 4–4–0 No.49 GORDON HIGHLANDER. Both locomotives now reside in the Glasgow Transport Museum at Kelvin Hall. For the exhibition, the booking office across the tracks on Benalder Street received a temporary facade in garishly coloured canvas. Passenger services and general goods traffic ceased together in 1964 but the yard off to the left still had private sidings serving on oil depot and scrap metal merchant until these were closed during 1978 because of work on the Argyle line.

A less exotic train, the 5.10 pm Dumbarton – Carmyle called at Kelvin Hall on 9th August 1960. Stanier class 3MT 2–6–2T No.40159 blasted through the drizzle past Spillers Scotstoun Mills and the gently decaying Partick Central signal cabin before plunging into Stobcross tunnel. The ornate factory stood on the site of an old water–powered mill, one reminder of which is a weir directly below the L & D bridge. This structure, of fish–bellied and plate girders resting on circular masonry piers, survives along with the station booking hall in this dank forgotten corner of Partick.

North Side Caledonian

Caledonian frustration with North British progress on the north bank of the Clyde was brought to a head by the Glasgow City & District. There had been a creeping penetration of the north side for nearly 40 years, beginning with the purchase of the Garnkirk line and the opening of Buchanan Street in 1849. A modest probing further south came with the Rutherglen – Dalmarnock branch of 1861 and in 1874 the Caley was begrudgingly allowed access to Queen's Dock over North British metals. This involved complicated manoeuvres through Sighthill yards, enforced delays crossing the Glasgow – Edinburgh main line at Cowlairs, and goods depots on the Stobcross branch deep in alien territory, so the arrangement was hardly satisfactory. A branch authorised from the Garnkirk line east of St. Rollox to the Forth & Clyde canal at Hamiltonhill in 1876 remained unbuilt, but it heralded later developments. Meanwhile passenger traffic began at London Road in the east end and Central station in the city centre during 1879. The London Road – Blochairn Junction goods line opened on 2nd August 1886, providing a link between the routes out of Central and Buchanan Street, but the Caley was still in no position to claim a real share of the lucrative mineral, goods and suburban passenger traffic which was mushrooming on the north bank.

All this changed in the mid–1890s with the completion of the Lanarkshire & Dumbartonshire Railway and Glasgow Central Railway, two nominally independent local lines with very heavy Caledonian backing, and the resurrection of the Hamiltonhill branch. The Lanarkshire & Dumbartonshire ran along the northern shore of the Clyde from Dumbarton to Stobcross via Bowling, Kilpatrick, Dalmuir, Clydebank, Yoker, Scotstoun and Partick. For much of the way it was only a couple of hundred yards from the river and was in an ideal position to serve the succession of wharfs, factories and shipyards which had grown up. There was also a steeply graded branch from Partick to Possil via Maryhill. At Possil Junction this joined the Hamiltonhill branch which started at Robroyston and Balornock Junctions on the Buchanan Street line and looped northwards through Springburn Park. The Glasgow Central Railway linked Dalmarnock with Maryhill via Bridgeton Cross, Glasgow Green, Glasgow Cross, Glasgow Central, Anderston Cross, Stobcross, Kelvin Bridge, Botanic Gardens and Kirklee. It was a remarkable railway, spending most of its passage through the city centre and western suburbs underground and incorporating Scotland's longest railway tunnel.

Although the L & D and GCR were promoted separately, they soon became one system from the operational point of view and were always worked by the Caledonian as an integral part of its own network. By 1896 the parent company had gained two routes from the collieries and ironworks of Lanarkshire to the engineering works and quays of north Clydeside, together with long awaited independent access to Queen's Dock. Comprehensive passenger services were also possible, shadowing the North British virtually every mile of the way. Dawsholm shed near Maryhill provided motive power for these routes until 1964. But after nearly 70 years of intensive use, the Caley's expensive north side network was becoming an anachronism as freight traffic ebbed away and the grimy steam hauled service compared very unfavourably with the 'Blue Trains' on parallel former North British lines. The whole system was abandoned in the 1960s.

LANARKSHIRE & DUMBARTONSHIRE

The original Lanarkshire & Dumbartonshire plan envisaged a line from the shore of Loch Lomond through Dumbarton to Stobcross on the Glasgow Central Railway, which had already been authorised. However, the prospect of rival steamer services on Loch Lomond together with a series of new passenger stations and industrial sidings next to its own facilities west of Partick hardly pleased the North British. Prolonged wrangling between the parties resulted in the abandonment of the proposed L & D Loch Lomond – Dumbarton section, transfer of the existing Balloch to Dumbarton line to joint ownership, and Caledonian access to an enlarged Dumbarton station. The L & D Act of 5th August 1891 also authorised the route from Partick to Possil. In reality this was three separate sections – Partick West to Bellshaugh Junction, Bellshaugh Junction to Maryhill Junction, and Maryhill station to Possil Junction – which together tied up the loose ends of the Glasgow Central Railway at Dawsholm and Maryhill and provided a connection with the Hamiltonhill branch.

The main line of the L & D began underground at a junction with the Glasgow Central Railway just west of Stobcross station. It pursued a low level course as far as Partick West and involved some ingenious engineering work. Immediately west of Stobcross station the L & D tunnelled beneath the high level sidings serving Queen's Dock and a peculiar smoke vent resembling a porthole punctured the southern wall, giving a fleeting glimpse of ships at the adjacent quayside. Difficult geological conditions hampered progress here, but a problem of a different kind was encountered a few hundred yards west of Partick

At Partick West the L & D assumed its distinctive course between side street tenements and commercial premises strung along the river bank. Shortly after Partick Central, trains faced a 1 in 80 climb through a curved cutting to reach the long embankment section to Dalmuir, and on 3rd August 1960 Fairburn 2–6–4T No.42244 breasted the gradient with the 5.35 pm Rutherglen to Balloch, watched by a trio of likely lads bound for town. Partick East Junction signal box in the background controlled the Possil line, curving away to the left together with a low level branch along South Street. The latter can be seen descending on the right behind posters extolling the delights of the West Highlands. Beyond it, Meadowside Quay contained several grain wagons, whilst the shipyard cranes of Govan pierced the skyline in the distance.

Central station. The L & D, in a vertical–walled cutting, passed below Vine Street at precisely the same point as the North British line from Queen Street Low Level crossed overhead at an acute angle. To guarantee stability, the latter's cast iron bridge supports had to be underpinned to a depth of 50ft. in what proved to be a very difficult operation. From Partick West to Dalmuir the line was largely on an embankment overlooking the river, although it was forced to veer inland at Clydebank to avoid the huge John Brown shipyard. Beyond Dalmuir the rails ran in open countryside alongside the increasingly attractive Clyde estuary and at Bowling crossed an impressive swingbridge across the Forth & Clyde Canal.

A steep climb faced the Possil branch as soon as it left Partick West and over the next four miles there were bridges over the River Kelvin and under the Forth & Clyde Canal, four tunnels, and all manner of earthworks and masonry. The L & D section from Possil Junction to Maryhill, together with the Hamiltonhill branch and the Glasgow Central Railway from Maryhill to Stobcross, opened for mineral traffic to Queen's Dock on 26th November 1894. Goods traffic over the Maryhill to Partick and Clydebank to Stobcross sections began on 1st May 1896, followed by Clydebank to Dumbarton on 15th June. Passenger services commenced on 1st October 1896. The L & D remained legally independent until absorbed by the Caledonian on 16th August 1909.

Until nationalisation the rival north bank companies were quite content to confuse passengers with identical names for different stations, but in early BR days many former L & D stations gained suffixes. Dalmuir, Clydebank and Whiteinch all had 'Riverside' added, Yoker changed to Yoker Ferry, and Maryhill sounded more important when it became Maryhill Central. In a single blow passenger services were withdrawn from the L & D system on 5th October 1964 – although Kelvinside and Crow Road stations on the Possil line had perished earlier and a short section east of Dumbarton had been incorporated in the electrified network at the expense of the parallel North British route. Goods yards at Yoker, Whiteinch and Maryhill finished in 1965 and the line down to Stobcross docks closed on 15th July 1968. The route through Possil and Maryhill to Partick closed completely on 22nd February 1966, although the formation was retained for possible reopening until 1983. The main line survived as a long siding from Yoker to Partick Central until 23rd October 1978 and a short section lingered on further west until traffic was withdrawn from Old Kilpatrick Naval Fuel Depot in March 1986, and Arnott Young Shipbreakers at Dalmuir in August 1987. Much earlier casualties had been the distinctive island platform stations with their attractive but unadaptable buildings. All were quickly demolished leaving the lovely stone structure at Kelvinside and the brick offices at Partick Central and Possil as the only reminders of the L & D.

Whiteinch Riverside was typical of the L & D's 'main line' stations. Its island platform stood on an embankment between South Street and Curle Street and the timber building displayed horizontal boarding, bay windows, and a modest amount of decorative woodwork over the doors. A generous canopy supported on lattice girders was capped by a low–pitched slate roof, whilst hanging gas lamps and attractive benches provided detail. St. Rollox Class 5 4–6–0 No.45155 with a rake of corridor stock (including a couple of new Mk1s in 'blood and custard' livery) added a touch of style to Whiteinch on 22nd April 1957. This Easter Monday excursion from Dalmuir Riverside to the Fife Coast resort of Leven had a helping heave from a Dawsholm Austerity up the bank from Maryhill to Robroyston.

The embankment carrying L & D metals from Partick West to Clydebank formed a barrier between Dumbarton Road and South Street. Numerous side streets linking the two had to be spanned and at Whiteinch there were no less than four plate girder bridges in ¼ of a mile. But this elevated passage also complicated rail access to the riverside engineering works and shipyards. The solution was the branch from Partick East Junction, which ran along South Street for nearly two miles. In the shadow of the main line embankment at Whiteinch, McIntosh 0–4–0ST No.56030 shepherded a few wagons along South Street on 22nd November 1955. The 75 year old Caley 'Pug', its running board warped by over–zealous shunting, was one of the unsung heroes of Glasgow's railways and a world apart from the express engines at Central station, just three miles away.

Despite a valiant effort, the waiting room chimney was no match for Austerity 2–8–0 No.90493 when it came to shrouding the environs of Scotstoun East in smoke. The train consisted of empty wagons returning from Rothesay Dock to the Lanarkshire coalfield, on 18th April 1956. The former North British terminus at Whiteinch Victoria Park was 200 yards away to the right and its associated tramway down to the river can be seen emerging from Scotstoun Street in front of Cairns Dairies corner shop.

This view of one of Dawsholm's Stanier 2–6–2Ts, No.40158, thumping away from Scotstoun East with the 4.28 pm Dalmuir Riverside – Rutherglen on 28th August 1958, is very evocative of the L & D during the 1950s. Considering the closeness of stations, local services were quite smartly timed and in 1958 trains covered the 6 miles from Dalmuir to Partick Central in 25 minutes with 7 intermediate stops. Despite the intention to run fast non–stop trains from Dumbarton to Glasgow, the L & D island platforms were approached by sharp curves, no doubt to economise on the amount of embankment required. The dour tenements of Fore Street stood guard over the station and factories in South Street can be seen on the far left.

Elderly Caledonian engines were used on light freight duties in the mid–1950s and Drummond 0–6–0 No.57429, disfigured by a stovepipe chimney, trundled through Yoker Ferry on 28th May 1956 with a string of coal empties it had collected from various sidings along the Dumbarton line. Yoker Ferry was one of the few brick–built L & D stations and being in a heavily industrialised area was probably the most grimy. The equally soot–caked tenements of Lasswade Street looked out over Rothesay Dock; formally opened on 25th April 1907, principally for coal exports, it can be seen on the left. It was reached by a 1½ mile branch from Scotstoun West that ran north of the L & D for a while before passing under Yoker Ferry station, directly below this viewpoint. A skew girder bridge carried the platform and running lines over the four dock tracks, and evidence of its construction can be clearly seen.

Back at Partick West, the triangular junction of the Possil line with the L & D main line had side platforms on the arm facing Glasgow, and on 3rd August 1960 Fairburn 2–6–4T No.42203 rolled into this part of the station with the 5.32 pm Possil – Whifflet Upper. The two spurs each had their own girder bridge across Dumbarton Road. Beyond here the ground rose sharply and despite a 1 in 76 gradient the line had to tunnel beneath the side streets of Partick for a ¼ mile before emerging at Crow Road. A wide cutting, overlooked by the tenements of Crathie Drive and Maule Drive but hidden behind high sandstone walls at street level, formed the tunnel approach.

Crow Road is the main route through Partick from Jordanhill to Dumbarton Road and although the station of that name was actually on nearby Clarence Drive, the choice of name was appropriate. A red brick booking hall with round–headed windows flanked by decorative stonework faced Clarence Drive; it was supported on girders across the Glasgow–bound track and cast iron columns set in the island platform. The standard L & D structure at the lower level was finished off with cream bricks above a glazed brown brick base, separated by a course of ornamental tiles. Colourful posters – this time of Loch Ness and the North East Coast – greeted the 5.19 pm Rutherglen – Possil, guided in by Standard 2–6–4T No.80002 on 9th September 1959. The station was a casualty of the Queen Street Low Level electrification and closed on 6th November 1960, when Hyndland's new facilities on the adjacent North British route opened.

Although it was little more than a mile in length, the Kelvinside – Maryhill section of the L & D was a complex stretch of railway both in terms of conception and construction. Immediately after Kelvinside station there was a tunnel which curved through almost 90 degrees under the edge of Kelvindale. Then came Bellshaugh Junction, where the line joined the Glasgow Central Railway's Dawsholm branch on a massive retaining wall high above the River Kelvin. After a couple of hundred yards it veered off on its own again across a curving viaduct over the river. In this view, looking south towards Great Western Road, Clayton Type 1 No.D8525 crossed the Kelvin with the 5.3 pm Rutherglen – Possil on 10th September 1963. Towards the end about half of the Central Low Level services were diesel operated. The Claytons were notorious for noise and fumes and were hardly an improvement on steam in the tunnels. They shared the work with English Electric Type 1s and Cravens diesel multiple units. The Glasgow Central line from Kirklee to Dawsholm is behind the train and the Kirklee – Maryhill tracks are off to the left on their own bridge. 'Greek' Thomson's terraces on Great Western Road are in the distance.

The half mile stretch between Crow Road and Kelvinside began in a cutting and continued through a short tunnel beneath the North British suburban line, originally the Stobcross branch, near Gartnavel Hospital – mainly uphill at 1 in 88. Kelvinside station was unique. It stood on Great Western Road little more than quarter of a mile from 'Greek' Thomson's Great Western Terrace, and Glasgow architect John Burnet produced a design wholly in harmony with the elegant neighbourhood. The square plan building, in pale sandstone, had delicately hipped roofs with wide eaves and featured strong string courses, notably on the chimneys. A balcony with a fine balustrade topped by two enormous urns graced the frontage. Unfortunately passenger receipts were meagre and it was closed from January 1917 to June 1919 as a World War 1 economy measure; it finally succumbed on 1st July 1942, a victim of World War 2. English Electric Type 1 No.D8080 passed moribund Kelvinside on 25th September 1964 with a southbound mineral train. Fortunately, after years of disuse, various attempts by BR to demolish it, and an arson attack, the listed structure was refurbished as a restaurant in 1983.

Possil station was on the northern extremity of the L & D, linking Maryhill with the Hamiltonhill branch at Possil Junction, and just 300 yards from Possilpark station on the North British Cowlairs – Helensburgh line. Passenger services had a hesitant start followed by a somewhat chequered career. Workmen's trains ran from 1st February 1897 but the extension of public services from Maryhill did not begin until 1st October. Advertised traffic ceased on 1st May 1908 and was not reinstated until 8th January 1934. Accommodation at Possil hardly reflected this uncertainty, for the large brick building fronting Balmore Road overlooked lengthy platforms, one of which featured a delightful little pavilion for waiting passengers. Although the through tracks had platforms for a circular service down to Rutherglen, this never materialised and the bay usually proved adequate. Drummond 0–6–0 No.57346 – scruffy yet still elegant, like its surroundings – waited to leave for central Glasgow in the mid–1950s. The street level building survived as an off licence and betting office into the 1980s. Photograph courtesy Neville Stead.

The Possil line was virtually a conveyor belt for coal and iron for most of its life but severe gradients along the route from Partick demanded very hard work from engines hauling loaded eastbound trains. The heavy iron ore workings from Rothesay Dock to Coatbridge, double headed by Dawsholm Austerities, were particularly spectacular. WD 2–8–0s Nos.90114 and 90193 with raw material for Gartsherrie Ironworks were well into the 1 in 77/1 in 97 bank from Maryhill to Springburn Park as they thundered over the Glasgow – Edinburgh main line on 16th July 1960, leaving the sky looking like a storm was about to break. The eight span plate girder bridge crossing the former North British tracks was removed early in 1980, quite a while after the line itself closed on 22nd February 1966. The Balornock Junction – London Road section of the sweeping freight line round the east of Glasgow succumbed earlier, on 7th September 1964.

Carving on Caledonian Mansions, near Kelvin Bridge.

GLASGOW CENTRAL RAILWAY

The Glasgow Central Railway was authorised three years earlier than the Lanarkshire & Dumbartonshire, on 10th August 1888, but building it was such an enormous task that the two lines opened more or less at the same time. Like the Glasgow City & District, it linked the crowded east end with the prosperous west end but penetrated the suburbs and city centre even more thoroughly, albeit at an enormous cost. Most of the track was in tunnels below Dalmarnock Road, London Road, Argyle Street, Kelvingrove Park, Great Western Road and Botanic Gardens. At the same time it was a line of anomalies, just like the city it served. Passengers had to endure

choking smoke in the dim and dismal environment below ground at most stations, yet at street level the GCR announced its presence by some of the most magnificent suburban railway architecture in Britain. Furthermore, at its extremities the Stygian low level route adopted an airy stance and featured lofty river bridges and even rural surroundings.

The Caley's cross–city line might have taken on a very different guise. In 1887 the Glasgow Central & Suburban Railway proposed an elevated line along a similar route and Argyle Street may well have looked like Wabash Street in Chicago had it not been for the public outrage and subsequent rethink. A year later the Glasgow Central Railway obtained parliamentary approval for its line from Dalmarnock to Maryhill and Dawsholm, this time largely underground. Land purchase was fraught with difficulties and construction work had still not started when the Caledonian absorbed the GCR on 31st May 1890. But by then legal difficulties had been sorted out and the hugely expensive six year business of actually building the railway began within a fortnight. A few weeks later, on 25th July 1890, the eastward extension from Bridgeton Cross to Newton via Carmyle gained parliamentary approval. This was a logical extension providing alternative access to the industrial areas of Coatbridge, Motherwell and Hamilton, thus relieving pressure on the main line.

In the middle section of the GCR it was necessary to excavate some of the busiest streets in Glasgow. Then, as now, they were lined with commercial premises and one of the many complications was the presence of tram tracks throughout. Disruption to business and transport alike had to be kept to the minimum. The Caledonian received considerable acclaim for the meticulous engineering work on its underground railway, but it was the sort of project only a very wealthy company could contemplate. Firstly, steel sheeting was driven down to the required depth either side of the roadway, using a gantry pile–driver to avoid obstructing traffic. Trenches were then excavated so that the tunnel walls could be built up, and the street surface was replaced by timber flooring to carry the tram lines. Sufficient earth was excavated below this to accommodate the deep cross–girders which were placed in position on Sundays when no trams were running. The intermediate roof space was then filled with brick arching and the permanent road surface reinstated. Finally, spoil was removed to complete the tunnel and a concrete 'invert' laid to form the floor.

Work proceeded section by section, but was rarely straightforward. The Clyde was only a few hundred yards away and at high tide water seeped into the workings. Patches of wet sand had to be excavated a little at a time, lined with timber, and the remaining crevices packed

The southern end of the Glasgow Central Railway was at Dalmarnock. It left the Rutherglen – London Road line at Strathclyde Junction and descended in a stone walled cutting before taking up an underground course below Dalmarnock Road as far as Bridgeton Cross. On 22nd July 1963 Fairburn 2–6–4T No.42208 lifted the 5.16 pm Dalmuir Riverside to Rutherglen into daylight ¾ mile from its destination. This view from Strathclyde Street bridge is a tableau of the area's railway history. On the right rows of wagons occupy the terminus of the 1861 branch from Rutherglen. In the centre the 1877 extension to London Road climbs across Dalmarnock Road, where there was a high level passenger station called Bridgeton from 1879 until the low level line opened in 1895. On the left sidings served various industrial premises, including Dalmarnock gasworks. Dalmarnock station, partly in tunnel and partly spanned by girders bracing the cutting walls, was abandoned in 1964 and revived with electrification in 1979. The nearby goods yard ceased to handle general traffic in September 1965 but became a 'Tartan Arrow' depot, lasting in turn until 1982. London Road goods closed in January 1984 and this meant the end of the high level tracks at Dalmarnock.

with coco fibre. Painstaking underpinning of adjoining buildings was also necessary; trenches were dug beneath the foundations, new brick and concrete supports built up, and iron wedges driven in to ensure stability. As if this was not enough, numerous primitive sewers draining down to the river were also encountered and had to be diverted into new channels below the line. As a result the tunnel actually had four underbridges including one over the long–culverted Molendinar Burn. By the time work finished it had taken 25,000 tons of steel, 70 million bricks, six years of relentless effort, and a lot of Caledonian cash to get the Glasgow Central Railway through the city centre.

Maryhill to Stobcross opened for mineral traffic to Queen's Dock on 26th November 1894 as noted earlier. A passenger service between Rutherglen and Glasgow Cross began on 1st November 1895 ending the Rutherglen – London Road shuttle, and the rest of the elegant GCR stations opened on 10th August 1896. Newton – Carmyle – Bridgeton Cross passenger trains began on 1st February 1897. The line was an immediate success with over 250 services a day passing through Glasgow Central Low Level, half of them from the Lanarkshire & Dumbartonshire route. Most trains consisted of six–wheel compartment coaches hauled by new McIntosh 0–4–4 tanks fitted with condensing gear for the tunnels. But the atmosphere underground was foul from the outset and the tramways, cossetted during construction work were soon electrified, to become a formidable competitor.

Despite the unfavourable conditions and fierce rivalry, the Caley underground line remained a fast and convenient route from the suburbs to the city centre for over 60 years. Timings were lively and not much different to the present electric service, so there was a relatively high use of the grimy steam trains even towards the end. In summer 1958 for example there were 36 westbound and 37 eastbound trains at Central Low Level with no less than 21 starting or finishing points. Services included Balloch – Law Junction, Strathaven – Possil, Kilbowie – Motherwell, Cumbernauld – Anderston Cross, Old Kilpatrick – Coatbridge and Carmyle – Maryhill, although Balloch – Rutherglen and vice versa accounted for about a quarter of the total.

In winter the underground smog was

John Burnet's highly embellished entrance building at Glasgow Cross station.

sometimes so thick that even the platforms were difficult to see. On a few occasions, notably at Glasgow Cross, passengers fell down on the ballast, deluded that they were at a platform when the train stopped short of the station. Inside the carriages, windows streamed with condensation and even the upholstery was damp – but this often seemed the situation on hot summer days as well. At

Between Newton and Carmyle the eastern extension of the Glasgow Central Railway traversed the Clyde valley by a sweeping reverse 'S' curve. In marked contrast to its claustrophobic passage through the city centre, the Caledonian low level line reached breezy heights here and spanned the river itself on hefty lattice deck girders, supported by tall sandstone piers. On 15th August 1963, three weeks after its appearance at Dalmarnock, No.42208 crossed the Clyde with a solitary parcels van from Hamilton. The signal box and semaphores controlled Westburn Junction, where the Lanarkshire & Ayrshire spur from Kirkhill came in. Timetabled passenger trains over this section of the L & A had always been spasmodic, but a regular service on the Newton – Carmyle line was maintained until 1964, albeit rather meagre towards the end. Daily freights from Carmyle to British Steel Cambuslang near Westburn Junction finished in May 1983 and the line over the bridge closed. Rail traffic from Newton to the Cambuslang works, by then known as Redpath Engineering, ceased in December 1989.

the front of the train exhaust beats from an engine travelling bunker first reverberated round the tunnel and could be deafening. For 60 years the line had mechanical signalling but smoke made the semaphores difficult to see and fumes shortened the life of equipment. Remarkably, there were few accidents. On 18th August 1952 there was a rear end collision between Dalmarnock and Bridgeton Cross due to 'serious irregularities' by a signalman, whilst on 31st January 1949 a driver ran past three signals at danger before hitting a stationary train at Glasgow Cross because of 'much smoke and steam hanging in the tunnels'. There were no serious injuries in these accidents, but on 22nd February 1939 one passenger had been killed in a collision at Stobcross. In the 1949 accident report the inspecting officer noted that 'ventilation on this underground line with its fairly dense traffic has been unsatisfactory for a long time... the obvious remedy would be the elimination of steam haulage'. Ironically on 2nd August 1898 the Caley had received parliamentary powers to electrify the Glasgow Central Railway but decided not to proceed. In 1956 multiple aspect colour lights controlled by panels at Bridgeton Cross and Stobcross replaced the semaphores and signal boxes at intermediate stations were abolished. Because the rails were invariably dirty a special feature supplemented the track circuiting. An electrically operated detonator placed in advance of each signal was only withdrawn when the signal cleared, and was immediately replaced once a train had passed.

Closure came on 5th October 1964 along with the Lanarkshire & Dumbartonshire, although by this time a number of stations had already given in to road competition. The whole formation was retained for possible reinstatement of services and the middle section

did indeed reopen as the Argyle line, 15 years later. Unfortunately finance for the eastern extension through Parkhead and the west end section from Stobcross to Maryhill was not forthcoming and building work has been allowed on the trackbed.

At Carmyle the new line briefly made use of the existing Rutherglen – Coatbridge branch by means of junctions at either end of the station. It then headed west through Tollcross and entered a long cutting overlooked by the tenements of Parkhead. A station was provided between the overbridges carrying Helenvale Street and Springfield Road and in March 1952 it was renamed Parkhead Stadium in recognition of its proximity to Celtic's ground. On 19th June 1963 the football club's floodlights dominated the skyline but there were no fans thronging the platforms on this sultry Wednesday evening, when Ivatt 4MT 2-6-0 No.43140 paused with the 5.6 pm Dalmuir Riverside to Coatbridge Central. The proud Caledonian buildings at street level and down on the platforms where even the chimneys displayed intricate decoration, had survived years of neglect. Closure was little more than a year away and the inhabitants of Whitby Street looked down on overgrown shrubs and broken canopy glass, making posters urging passengers to put their litter in the bins seem somewhat futile.

Beyond Parkhead the Newton arm of the Glasgow Central Railway also went underground, this time below London Road. At Bridgeton Cross the tunnels opened out and the two routes converged. Trains from Dalmarnock used the platform on the right, where Fairburn 2-6-4T No.42058 waited with the 3.40 pm Rutherglen – Dalmuir Riverside on Friday 25th September 1964. A torrential downpour added gloom to the careworn surroundings ten days before closure. Services from Newton and Carmyle used the island platform on the left, where the eastbound track was still below London Road. When the lines opened Bridgeton was already an important satellite of Glasgow and had been served by the North British branch from High Street since 1892. Six roads converged between the two stations and an elegant cast iron gazebo with a little clock tower known as the 'Umbrella' has been a focal point for over a century.

Central Low Level was a huge brick and metal cave 960 feet long and 120 feet wide, with two island platforms serving four tracks. Walls twelve feet thick and a series of hefty columns with bulbous bases supported the overhead girders. Access from Argyle Street and the main line station was via a labyrinth of passageways lined with glazed white bricks where small illuminated indicators announced the next service. If a winter smog gripped Glasgow, conditions on the platforms could be oppressive, and tiny pools of light emanating from the hanging lamps lit up nothing more than smoke. Photography was very difficult and illustrations are extremely rare. This study of a Stanier 2–6–2T hauling LMS compartment stock shows a scene repeated hundreds of times a week in the 1950s, yet virtually unrecorded. Steam from the safety valves is scouring soot off the roof and distributing it liberally, just to add to the general discomfort! Photograph H.C. Casserley.

Glasgow Cross station was completely underground and a small wedge–shaped vent did little to let out the fumes. The railway presence at street level was much more in tune with its surroundings and architect John Burnet's bulbous octagonal building, capped by a squat dome, had a vague affinity with the top of the nearby Tolbooth. It had to come down for road improvements in the early 1920s, but at least its plainer replacement was solid and dignified. This was prominent on the right as Coronation tram No.1255, en route to Auchenshuggle, left the Tron Steeple behind on 11th August 1962. Although closed to passengers in 1964 the building was not demolished until 1977, when preparatory work for the Argyle line was underway. The station itself did not reopen and new facilities were provided beyond Tron Steeple instead.

After Bridgeton Cross the line went underground again and Glasgow Green station was basically just a gap in the tunnel roof dominated by the massive rear wall of Templeton's carpet factory. Stairways led to the booking office facing Binnie Place and the broad vista of Glasgow Green sweeping down to the Clyde was revealed. Next to the station Templeton's presented an astonishing face to the Green. This riotous concoction of red brick gothic, set off by blue, green and cream mosaics, was based on the Doge's Palace in Venice and has to be seen to be believed. Glasgow Green station eventually succumbed to the trams on 2nd November 1953, but the frontage with its name picked out in gilt letters on red sandstone still complements one of the world's most exotic factories. Photograph Paul Anderson.

Anderston Cross station was another good example of impressive surface facilities contrasting with an unappealing environment at rail level. There was little scope for fine architecture below ground although the columns boasted lavishly decorated capitals and there was the usual intricate Caledonian woodwork. John Burnet's street level building was a tall two storey edifice with a curving sandstone facade, combining solid dignity with vigorous Baroque decoration. Standard tram No.270 waited at the terminus of route 15 outside the station on 22nd July 1959. Anderston Cross lost its trains less than two weeks later on 3rd August, but the trams continued until 10th March 1962. Since then the area has been totally transformed by the M8 motorway on its approach to Kingston Bridge. Reopening as plain Anderston took place in 1979 but the booking office is now just a small brick building under a slip road. Nevertheless a certain amount of the original atmosphere remains at platform level.

Beyond Anderston Cross the line finally deserted Argyle Street – which veered off towards Partick – and tunnelled beneath Stobcross Street for a further half mile to reach Stobcross station. Here, enough light came through a side vent to show the roof structure of the underground stations. The supporting columns were intermediate in size and the configuration of girders was determined by roadways and other features above. Evening sunshine also revealed how shabby the Glasgow Central Railway had become, as Fairburn class 4MT 2–6–4T No.42200 rolled into the western end of the station with the 5.15 pm Balloch to Rutherglen on 23rd July 1959. The crossover enabled goods trains from the Maryhill line to gain access to Queen's Dock. Stobcross closed along with Anderston Cross on 3rd August 1959 but its derelict buildings and platforms remained intact until the 1970s. It was rebuilt further west as part of the Argyle Line project, opening as Finnieston in 1979. It was renamed Exhibition Centre in 1986.

Stanier 2-6-2T No.40152 momentarily basked in sunlight at the east end of Stobcross station with the 5.16 pm Dalmuir Riverside – Carmyle on 23rd July 1959. From Stobcross the Glasgow Central tracks swung north towards the west end, and tunnelling continued unabated under Finnieston and Kelvingrove Park. The tunnel ended where Eldon Street spanned the river by a decorative iron bridge. This was the first substantial open air section since Dalmarnock and the line was in a virtual amphitheatre, with the fretwork spire of the University peeping over the roof line from the west. Kelvin Bridge passenger station was tucked away in a corner, overlooked by the fine railway–built Caledonian Mansions. Another long tunnel section began here and the portal featured monumental stonework in harmony with the Mansions and an even more ornate metal bridge, where Great Western Road crossed the Kelvin.

GCR tracks passed below Great Western Road for nearly half a mile until they encountered Botanic Gardens. The Glasgow Botanic Institution demanded an ornamental station and the result was one of Britain's most exotic suburban railway buildings, where architect James Miller clearly let his imagination run wild. Tall Tudor chimneys, half–timbered gables, a delicate veranda, and a little dormer window were delightful details. But it was the tapering towers, each clad with tiles, adorned with a clock in one instance and a medallion in the other, and capped by a balcony, lantern and onion–shaped dome in gleaming gold, which really gave the building its character. The station closed on 6th February 1939, but was still being used for other purposes as Dalmarnock–bound Standard car No.288 made its way along Great Western Road on 16th January 1960.

Rising ground made the Caledonian abandon 'cut and cover' and resort to conventional tunnelling for the first time on the Glasgow Central Railway, the changeover taking place below the Botanic Gardens grass. Trains emerged in a deep cutting carved out of the steep banks of the River Kelvin and the portal was the best on the line. Its large chiselled blocks of sandstone were set off by a decorative parapet and graceful curved retaining walls. Just beyond was Kirklee station. Considering the nature of the line so far this was an almost unbelievably sylvan setting, with trees all around and the sound of rushing water. It was once the site of Three Tree Well, where young Victorian lovers plighted their troths, but the railway destroyed it. John Burnet designed delightful station buildings to match the rural environment. In pouring rain on 24th October 1959 Stanier 2–6–2T No.40189 headed past Kirklee with the 9.54 am Law Junction to Maryhill Central./

Maryhill station was originally planned as one of the two northern termini of the Glasgow Central Railway, although it emerged as a significant place on the Lanarkshire & Dumbartonshire as well. On 10th September 1963 Fairburn 2–6–4T No.42208 from Motherwell shed waited in one of the bays with the 5.35 pm to Whifflet Upper. The Forth & Clyde Canal crossed the line in the distance beyond the bridge carrying Maryhill Road. Following the end of passenger services in 1964 every trace of the station was swept away, but when a large Co–Op supermarket was built on the site some 15 years later space was reserved in the basement for a single platform terminus. With the impending reinstatement of passenger services to the former North British station on the other side of Maryhill this was a wasted move.

One of the most unpromising locations for a suburban terminus in Britain, let alone Glasgow, was on the edge of Maryhill. It was called Dawsholm after the park to the north and was reached by ¾ mile of very expensive track. For a while the line ran above the Kelvin gorge on a massive retaining wall, to pass high above the river on two girder spans at a very acute angle. A viaduct followed by a plate girder bridge over Kelvindale Road carried the line to a shelf on the east bank of the river. Dawsholm station had an island platform sheltered by a long canopy supported on pairs of columns. It was meant to serve the northern side of Maryhill but access via a steep path from Bantaskin Street and through one of the arches of the Forth & Clyde Canal aqueduct was hardly convenient and passenger services ceased on 1st May 1908. The loco shed and branches to Dawsholm Gasworks, Temple Gasworks and Kelvindale Paperworks ensured its survival however. A brakevan rail tour headed by ex–NB class J37 0–6–0 No.64623 called at Dawsholm on 27th March 1964.

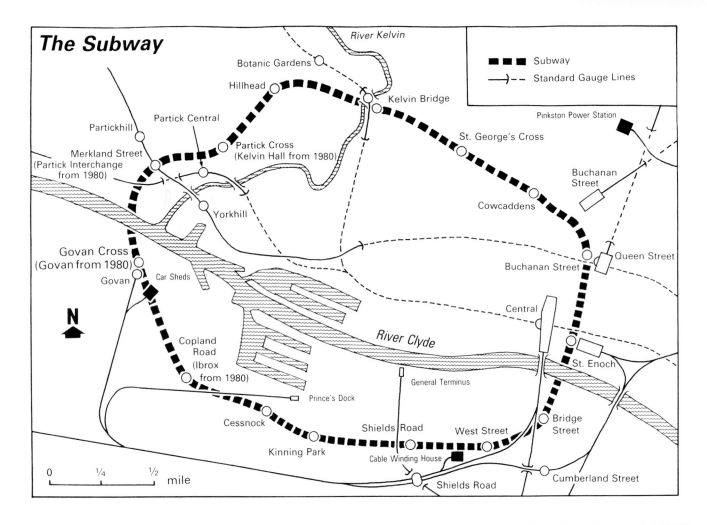

The Subway

Subway ▪▪▪▪
Standard Gauge Lines

River Kelvin

Botanic Gardens
Hillhead
Kelvin Bridge
Partickhill
Partick Central
St. George's Cross
Merkland Street
(Partick Interchange from 1980)
Partick Cross
(Kelvin Hall from 1980)
Pinkston Power Station
Buchanan Street
Cowcaddens
Yorkhill
Govan Cross
(Govan from 1980)
Car Sheds
Queen Street
Buchanan Street
Govan
Central
Copland Road
(Ibrox from 1980)
River Clyde
St. Enoch
Prince's Dock
General Terminus
Cessnock
Shields Road
West Street
Bridge Street
Kinning Park
Cable Winding House
Cumberland Street
Shields Road

N

0   ¼   ½   mile

Cowcaddens was typical of the less opulent examples of Glasgow Underground station entrances. The 1935 lettering and a touch of Art Deco ironwork hardly disguised the fact that it was basically a hole in a tenement block between the local drinking establishment and a shop. The former, with delicious impudence, clearly had no intention of acknowledging the Corporation attempts to bury the old Subway image! Standard car No.9 headed west along Cowcaddens Road on the way from Tollcross to Maryhill on 13th September 1960, a year before service 29 was replaced by bus route 61. The tenements have since been swept away and the station is now a small brick building dominated by new roads. Another victim of modernisation was the peculiar odour which pervaded the Underground stations. It was compounded, so it has been said, of damp and a substance called Stockholm Tar which was used to lubricate the cable.

The Subway

Near Queen Street and Central respectively the North British and Caledonian underground lines passed above the unique 4ft. gauge Glasgow Subway. Its name was an echo of New York but the diminutive cars became as much of a Glasgow institution as the trams or the Cathcart Circle. Although the City & District had made travelling easier from the western suburbs and the east end to the heart of the city and the Glasgow Central Railway promised to do the same, there was still a pressing need for improved transport within the central area in 1890. Surface railways had made no impact on the chronic congestion caused by horse drawn vehicles and furthermore the shipyards and streets of tenements immediately south of the Clyde needed a better link with the north bank. Consequently, on 4th August 1890 the Glasgow District Subway Company (changed to the Glasgow Subway Railway Company in 1914 for legal reasons) was given authority to build a 6½ mile circular route from St. Enoch to Bridge Street, Kinning Park, Govan, Hillhead and Kelvin Bridge then back to Buchanan Street. The scheme was warmly welcomed al-though there were exceptions – the Subway company had hoped to run below Great Western Road near Botanic Gardens but the Caledonian claimed the ground first. Steam traction was clearly out of the question, yet despite the choice of electricity for the pioneering City & South London tube, which opened in December 1890, the Glasgow line selected cable traction – made famous by the San Francisco cable cars from 1873 onwards.

Construction work started just outside the main line terminus at St. Enoch which was particularly apt in view of the subsequent success of the Subway and collapse of G & SW inner suburban traffic. Almost immediately the underground contractors experienced problems with waterlogged sand below St. Enoch's Square. Cutting shields backed by compressed air were employed and a couple of hundred yards further south the air pressure caused no less than ten blow–outs through the bed of the Clyde. A particularly spectacular one in February 1894 blasted timber staging out of a 24ft. hole and high above the water, causing panic among sailors on a nearby ship. Numerous workers succumbed to the damp pressurised environment and there were several fires underground. Even in the easier 'cut and cover' sections south of the river there were endless claims for compensation from property owners, including several dubious claims for redecoration. After well over £1½ million had been spent the Glasgow & District Subway opened on 14th December 1896 and there was a deluge of people eager to part with one penny at the turnstiles, to experience the novelty of travelling in 11ft. diameter tubes beneath the streets. Unfortunately the system had to be shut down following a serious collision about 11 pm, by which time one eager soul had been riding the cars for six hours.

Services were resumed on 21st January 1897 and Glaswegians flocked back underground, but this time all went well. By 1899 the cars were carrying 11 million passengers a year and the Subway prospered. Patronage remained at this level however, mainly because the newly electrified tramways above were absorbing the rapidly increasing demand for local transport. Costs were rising at the same time and by 1921 the company was in serious trouble. Furthermore it had become a bit of a

Fifteen stations were provided on the Subway. Generally, those north of the river were some way below street level whilst those on the south side were near the surface, and several even had glazed roofs. Most station entrances were barely noticeable although West Street and Copland Road had separate buildings and St. Enoch, the headquarters of the Subway Company, was a little gem. It was designed by James Miller and was constructed of red sandstone. Basically it consisted of a tall rectangular block with plain Tudor windows and a steeply pitched roof, but richly embellished gable ends and round corner turrets, each with bell–like cap and prominent weather vane, gave the building immense character. Intricate carving below the oriel window, surrounding the clock and on the projecting balcony, added further interest. Certain features such as the tall chimney were reminiscent of Miller's work on the Glasgow Central Railway. Queues similar to those on the opening day sometimes built up on Saturday afternoons when there were football fixtures at Ibrox, as on 23rd November 1957. Electrification had given rise to the UndergrounD lettering, which was a weak imitation of the contemporary London style, and also the rather tacky canopy. The building is now a Travel Centre and an escalator off to the right provides access to the platforms.

Beyond the nondescript doorway which greeted passengers at most stations there was a tiny ticket office window and a gloomy stairway down to the narrow island platform. These were made of timber in cable days and originally the station side walls were whitewashed. With electrification the platforms were rebuilt in concrete, the somersault starting signals at the tunnel mouths were replaced by colour lights and everywhere was generally brightened up. Copland Road still looked fairly cheerful on 13th April 1957 as a small group of passengers obeyed the 'Wait Here' marks on the platform and cars Nos.20 and 10 arrived with an Inner Circle train. Kinning Park station was the shallowest with just a 14ft. descent to the platform whilst Buchanan Street was the deepest, 82 steps leading down 40ft. The tunnels themselves were a mere 7ft. below the surface between Cessnock and Kinning Park but 155ft. beneath Glasgow Street, Hillhead. Gradients were as steep as 1 in 18 where the line plunged beneath the Clyde. Copland Road station was renamed Ibrox during the recent rebuilding and provided with both side and island platforms to deal with crowds for Rangers home games.

Early Subway publicity included a delightful poster showing passengers on a broad platform gazing up at a train and others sitting inside a carriage dwarfed by the ample dimensions of the vehicle. In reality the cars were just 7ft. 6in. wide and most people on the platforms came up to roof level. Nevertheless in their original form the coach interiors displayed typical late Victorian opulence. End panels were polished teak, the half partitions in the middle had stained glass windows and the longitudinal seating consisted of alternative birch and mahogany slats. The exterior livery was plum and cream. Under Corporation ownership the cars were painted red and cream, until 1954 when all–over red was adopted. Bucket seats in red or brown leather replaced the wooden benches when the carriages were refurbished for electrification, but the original folding iron lattice doors were retained. These were gradually displaced by solid sliding doors during the 1950s. Car No.28, proudly bearing the Glasgow coat–of–arms flanked by the municipal logo 'Corporation Transport' was being lifted by the overhead crane at Broomloan Road depot in Govan on 25th May 1958. Broomloan Road undertook all maintenance except foundry work and the 22½ ton hoist was the only means of getting coaches out of the tunnels. At night trains were stabled on the running tracks below Govan.

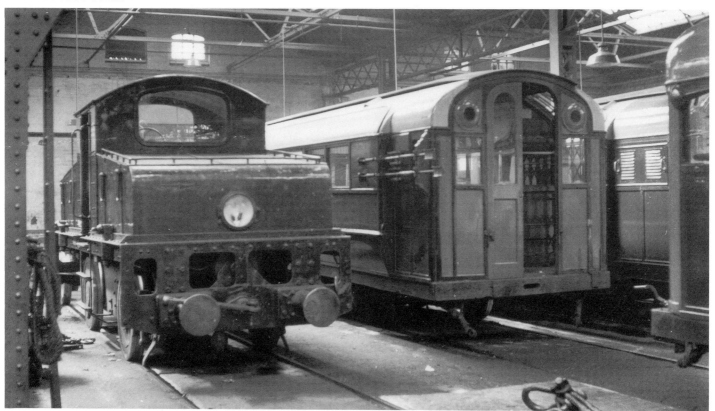

Elsewhere in Broomloan Road car sheds on 25th May 1958 was the Corporation's battery locomotive, used on maintenance trains in the tunnels.

joke. The impressive machinery in the engine house at Scotland Street and the skills required in keeping the continuous cables running were not apparent to the public – it was the uncomfortable jerk as cars gripped the cable on leaving a station that people noticed. Glasgow Corporation worked the system from July 1922 and purchased it outright on 1st August 1923. Modernisation was essential and electric traction, utilising the original cars equipped with motors, commenced on 31st March 1935 for the Inner Circle and the following 5th December for the Outer Circle. Running speed rose from 12 mph to 22 mph and passenger numbers soon increased to around 15 million a year. At the same time the Subway officially became the Underground in an attempt to bury the cable car stigma.

During 1954 the Corporation considered building branch lines to new housing estates, but at a cost of £4 million a mile for tunnelling this was hardly viable. Instead the two circles carried on much as before, except that they were now conveying around 30 million passengers a year. Twenty years later every aspect of the system was showing its age and the side walls of most coaches showed an alarming tendency to move in relation to the floor when at speed. Closure or complete reconstruction were the only options and happily the latter was chosen. The revitalised Glasgow Underground opened on 16th April 1980 after £60 million had been spent and the new trains with their bulbous contours and distinctive Strathclyde livery soon acquired the 'Clockwork Orange' nickname. Nevertheless, despite the efforts to stifle it 60 years ago, the title 'Subway' persists and is in remarkably common use.

Given a different twist of fate, local transport on Clydeside and elsewhere might look like this today. Long before steam succumbed to diesel and electric traction, there were several experiments in railway technology. One of the more bizarre efforts was the George Bennie Railplane, from a wealthy Glasgow engineer turned inventor. His airship–shaped cars with Pullman style furnishings hung from overhead tracks 16 feet above the ground and the propellers at each end were capable of whisking passengers along at 120 mph. With LNER co–operation a demonstration track was erected at Milngavie during June 1930. Initially it generated a lot of interest, but the idea never got off the ground (as it were!) and the derelict gantry was demolished in the early 1950s following Bennie's death, having somewhat amazingly survived the wartime scrap metal drive. Photograph W.A.C. Smith Collection.

ACKNOWLEDGEMENTS
The authors would like to thank F.W. Shuttleworth for processing the photographs. All are the copyright of W.A.C. Smith unless otherwise credited. They also wish to thank Barry Osborn of Leicester for typesetting the maps and Allison Bennett, also of Leicester, for photocopying work. Finally, thanks to Margaret Blackburn of Paisley Museum and Central Library for providing the Barrhead Central photograph.